The Defending Officer's Dog

Jack Cripps

THE DEFENDING OFFICER'S DOG
A Royal Engineer abroad in the Second World War

illustrated by Rose Shawe-Taylor

Millrace

First published in Great Britain in 2006 by
Millrace
2a Leafield Road, Disley
Cheshire SK12 2JF
www.millracebooks.co.uk

© 2006 The estate of J H H Cripps
Illustrations © 2006 Rose Shawe-Taylor

ISBN: 978-1-902173-21-4

Typeset in Adobe Garamond Pro.
Printed and bound in the United Kingdom
by MPG Books Ltd, Victoria Square, Bodmin, Cornwall.

Jack Cripps, c 1942

The author was characteristically enthusiastic about the proposal by Millrace to publish the wartime section of his memoir. Though he died before it could be finalised, his family and executors were keen that the project should go ahead as a tribute to him. The text has been edited as lightly as possible and the words and phrases in Kiswahili have been left exactly as Jack wrote them.

Contents

Introduction

This is a war memoir with a difference—a lively, unaffected account which focuses on aspects of the Second World War seldom in the spotlight. Jack Cripps was a young, unsophisticated officer in the Royal Engineers when he was sent to Kenya in 1942 to train African troops for Burma. He never saw combat (the war ended soon after his division finally reached north-east India) but the challenges of the job and his own adventurous nature led him into some remarkable situations. The narrative cuts between the serious and the riotous, from disarming a beserk askari to rickshaw-racing, from driving a truck-load of volatile wet gelignite to bicycling round a crowded dance floor at Lord Mountbatten's headquarters in Kandy. The backgrounds are defly drawn: Durban beaches, the cedar forests of Mount Kenya, the fleshpots of Mogadishu, the Ogaden desert, coconut plantations in Ceylon, a bridging camp on the Ganges.

Until he arrived in Mombasa, Jack had been hoping to join a front-line unit. Although disappointed to find instead that he had to build a camp and turn 800 untrained askaris into combat engineers, he set about it with characteristic eagerness. He learned Kiswahili and gradually developed a rapport with his troops. In his spare time, he established a pattern of activities that would later help him endure stifling, frustrating months in Ceylon and the Indian jungle: he explored as much as he could of the countryside and studied the wildlife. Slowly, the fascination of Africa took hold of him. There were other diversions, too. Shyly susceptible to pretty girls, he danced and played squash with Mary at the Nanyuki Club, partied at Delia's farm and fell in love with Ann during dawn rides on the slopes of Mount Kenya. His most important friend and companion, however, was Mick, an engaging half-breed dog. Mick is the star of several episodes, most memorably gatecrashing a court martial.

The chapters published here form the central part of a memoir Jack wrote for his grandchildren, to give them an understanding of the influences that made him who he was and the times he grew up in—a period almost incomprehensible to the children of a multicultural, technologically-obsessed and far less class-dominated era. He recognised that his generation had seen change unimaginable to any before or since:

> When I was born, cars were owned by the very few, commercial flying did not exist, man- and horse-power were responsible for at least ninety per cent of farm energy. The rest was steam. […] People were rigidly divided into aristocracy, professional and working

classes, with very little overlapping. What's more, they were as easily distinguishable by dress and manner of speaking as if they had worn labels. [...] Despite the obscene carnage of the 1914-18 war, which appeared to some to be the inevitable outcome of feudal thought, there seemed to others no reason why that same feudal system should not continue for ever.*

Jack's father, Henry Harrison Cripps (Harry), had experienced that carnage first hand. He was one of only a handful of his battalion of Royal Fusiliers to survive the Gallipoli landings and was later badly wounded at the Somme. His horrific experiences made him a withdrawn, private man who found it difficult to form close relationships. When he was discharged from hospital and stationed at Carrickfergus, however, he met Hilda Barbour Pring and they married shortly before the war ended. It was an unexpected but successful match. Hilda was just nineteen, the fourth of seven daughters of an Ulster manufacturer; she would later be remembered for a formidable mix of charm, eccentricity and determination.

Their first child, Blanche, was born in 1919 while Harry was with his regiment in India. Hilda took the baby out to join him a few months later but they were in London again for Jack's birth on Easter Sunday 1922. Brother and sister became and remained great friends and allies,

*All the quotations in this introduction are taken from the early chapters of Jack's memoir.

though Blanche's desire to take care of her little brother was frequently stretched to the limit by his apparent lack of physical fear. One incident, recalled by Jack with characteristic understatement, took place in 1927 in Königstein, where their father was stationed with the post-war army of occupation.

> *Now the dog next door was a large and very aggressive bitch that, we gathered, had already savaged several people. She lived on a short leash by her kennel which was not far from our door. In due course she and I made friends to such an extent that I had an open invitation into her kennel and, once there, woe betide anyone who tried to get me away from her protection. I soon learnt the political and military maxim of negotiation from strength. When, as often happened, my parents were particularly unreasonable, I would visit my friend and only agree to return when the negotiated reward was acceptably large.*

Blanche and Jack suffered the traditional fate of army offspring: constantly having to adapt to new environments and leave behind old friends. By 1928 they were back in Britain at the Royal Fusilier Depot at Hounslow, then still in the country. A rough gravel lane led from the barrack gates to several farms and the children were given a great deal of freedom to roam. They explored the area on bicycles and investigated the Heath, 'a real small boy's paradise, a wild and usually deserted place, full of mystery in the form of humps and hollows, old trenches, ruined tanks and other detritus of military training'. At the barracks, Jack was given riding lessons under the auspices of Cavalry Instructor Regimental Sergeant Major Grotti, of the 17th/21st Lancers, and a lifelong enthusiasm began.

> *The system was, as with cavalry recruits, to start in the riding school on a very large and quiet charger, fitted with a substantial neck strap on to which you held while the horse responded to the RSM's shouted instructions. When you were judged to have sufficient confidence at the various speeds, then the same horse took you over enormous jumps. In fact it wasn't even necessary to hold on to the strap, as my charger was like an armchair with kangaroo legs. In due course I acquired ample confidence and should have then gone on to the next stage of three gruelling years of cavalry drill (certainly under a less civilised RSM). Mercifully, I was spared this and rode happily ever after with a great deal of enthusiasm, but sadly lacking in elegance.*

Years later, in Kenya, he mastered the art of playing polo with the same gusto and lack of finesse.

This happy, untrammelled existence came to an abrupt end for Jack in 1929 when his parents sent him to a prep school, St Neots. Looking back, he reflected that he might have been allowed another year at home, had it not been for his tendency to bring home children of 'other ranks' as friends: 'My father was by now Commanding Officer of the Royal Fusilier Depot in the barracks, so I suppose my disregard of social barriers was a bit awkward…' As it was, at the time and for long afterwards, Jack was convinced that he had been rejected by his mother and was wretchedly unhappy. The lack of freedom at St Neots oppressed him, too, turning him into a rebel who broke bounds to explore the forbidden countryside beyond the school walls.

There were secret paths leading to beds of wild strawberries, there were trees to climb, deep ditches and mysterious ponds where lived frogs, newts and grass snakes, patches of dry heath where you could guarantee, on a warm day, to find lizards and adders. Then there was the ram [a pump] *which I could watch for hours. This was fed by a little runnel into which reddish brown water drained out of the bog (a favourite haunt of frogs) and, as if by magic connected with a weird regular metallic bump, water somehow found its way into storage tanks in the house.*

Such distractions may have fostered Jack's early interest in wildlife and engineering but otherwise his prep-school experience was bleak, lightened only by holidays with Blanche. He became something of a loner, shy, diffident and lacking in confidence. After St Neots, Marlborough College was a revelation, allowing unheard-of freedoms and possibilities. He could cycle to Savernake Forest, climb towering beech trees, watch the wildlife, swim in gravel pits and tickle trout. Huge circular pits in the ground provided walls of death for intrepid cyclists and he also became rather good at boxing. Then there was running on the downs, which yielded an uplifting, almost spiritual sensation that he was to recapture on a night exercise on Mount Kenya.

> *I particularly loved running in the wind and the rain, just holding a pace to keep that inner warmth. Sometimes, when I was really fit, I had a sense of weightlessness as if floating, without effort, while the ground rushed by beneath.*

Less appealing were the more formal demands of the school's OTC, where Jack's disdain for showy heroics did not go down well. He was given a section of twelve men and the task of 'attacking' an isolated bush on the downs, known to contain an enemy machine gun position.

> *I knew perfectly well what, in the Dad's Army tradition, was required of me, i.e. to provide some covering fire and then heroically to lead the rest of my men from infrequent bush to bush and receive, no doubt, a posthumous VC. Well, perhaps I valued my own and my men's lives too highly, or had just read about the appalling carnage on the Somme and at Passchendaele. At any rate, my suggestion of sending back a message to my Platoon commander who with a few rounds of the mortar in his possession could have eliminated the machine gun with absolutely no English casualties was not accepted.*

In 1937, Jack's parents and Blanche were out in India with the First Battalion Royal Fusiliers—his father's last command before retiring. Hilda decided that their son should join them in Delhi for a few months. Employing her extensive powers of persuasion on the Master of Marlborough, she convinced him that it would be good for Jack to take a term off school. It was his first experience of travel beyond northern Europe and he was enthralled and appalled by India. The breathtaking variety, the gorgeous palaces and the pleasure of early-morning rides with Blanche on their father's polo ponies contrasted with a nightmare experience that was supposed to be a special treat: he was taken along on a duck shoot.

As we reached the water, the first suspicion of dawn was just breaking and by the time we were in position in cold, waist-deep water, the eastern horizon showed as a thin glow of pink. The faint duck noises and distant honking of geese grew in a crescendo, then the whirring of wings as little groups of duck could just be made out above great skeins of geese. It was a brief moment of unforgettable magic and beauty, all too soon shattered. As dawn began to break, so the guns opened up and these beautiful, graceful creatures began to crumple and crash into the water. But there was even worse to come. We were killing far more birds than we could possibly eat or keep fresh in an Indian summer, so several local young men had volunteered to

*retrieve for us, on the understanding that they could
keep any surplus. Being Muslims they could only eat
birds which had died by having their throats cut by a
member of the faithful. The gruesome result was that
by the time the morning flight was over we were standing up to our waists in a lake of the blood of 200 ducks
and geese. I was sick with horror and shame.*

His reaction anticipated his later anger at the thoughtless
cruelty of his NCOs: 'How could depriving hundreds of
gloriously coloured and graceful birds of their life be called
sport?'

Accompanied by a pet mongoose, the family returned
to England in the troopship Dilwarra. In line with their
officer status, they travelled in luxury. Jack, observing that
he 'must have inherited many of the Cripps' socialist tendencies' (his father was a first cousin of Sir Stafford and a
nephew of Beatrice Webb) was horrified by the contrast
between their accommodation and that of the other ranks.
At Suez, he and his father took a train to Cairo, where
they viewed Tutankhamen's treasures and Jack, the future
engineer, scrutinised the construction of the Pyramids.

Despite his unconventional reaction to certain class
distinctions and pastimes, he was still the product of his
upbringing and background. He felt a surge of patriotic
pleasure on arriving back in Southampton.

*One was proud to be British [...] The Empire was
an accepted fact and [...] hopefully some day I should*

9

acquire the necessary qualities to take my place in the
ruling elite, but certainly not yet.

That 'yet' was to come sooner than he could have imagined and by the time he returned from wartime service his views would have changed radically. Meanwhile, his parents bought a rambling, beautiful house near Earls Colne in Essex. It was paradise to have a settled home.

Only a service child would understand what Bagga-
retts meant to me; something permanent that would be
the family's and then mine for ever. I loved the woods
and the bits of wilderness and soon knew every tree
and pond and ditch. I would spend hours wandering
round 'my estate' with a gun but only shooting when
Mother had asked for something for the pot. At last I
felt that here was somewhere where I belonged.

Having, despite the term off, passed his School Certificate, Jack was at back at Marlborough working for his Cambridge entrance exam when war was declared. His father, still only 53 and bored by retirement, was delighted to be recalled to take charge of the Royal Fusilier Training Depot at Hounslow. Even so, Jack felt that he could not now expect his parents to support him through an engineering degree course at university. Income tax was at fifty per cent, investment income had plummeted and there was Baggaretts to maintain. Since things seemed very quiet on the war front, he arranged an apprenticeship with a marine diesel firm in Greenock, to start when he left school.

The situation changed dramatically in May 1940. Hitler launched his Western Offensive, Chamberlain was replaced by Churchill as Prime Minister and the Netherlands fell. At the end of the month, the evacuation from Dunkirk began and by mid June the German army was in Paris. It no longer seemed the time to start an apprenticeship. Turned down by the RAF because his eyesight was not up to flying duty standard, Jack applied for the Royal Engineer course.

> *I duly appeared at an army medical examination. I went round a series of eight or nine cubicles in various stages of undress and seemed to have every conceivable system examined (donating specimens when required). I then proceeded to the table where sat the Colonel and his clerk. Without apparently examining the reports, the Colonel asked me if I was fit. On my answering 'Yes', I was awarded an A1 certificate and in due course enlisted in the Royal Engineers, taking the oath to serve His Majesty King George VI and his successors, until such a time as he would no longer require me...*

Since His Majesty did not require him until October, Jack bicycled with his friend John Shipster* to Devon to work in a forestry camp consisting entirely of ex-Marlburians. Because of his impending RE status, he was given the task of shoring up ancient bridges over the fast-flowing

Author of Mist on the Rice Fields, *about the Burma Campaign.*

river Exe. By the time he left, the Battle of Britain was raging. He was issued with uniform and despatched to Cambridge for a six-month course at Trinity Hall but it turned out to be of little value. Having been exempted the first year of the Mechanical Sciences Tripos, the exam for which the army course was working, he was pushed into second year work. Without a tutor, progress was slow and, in any case, they had to spend a great deal of time 'playing soldiers, including sitting half the night in a slit trench guarding the University library. (Against whom, or what we were to do with them, we were not quite clear.)'

In the spring of 1941, the course over, he was posted to the 3rd Training Battalion RE at Ripon for primary training ('It was hell and was meant to be') before arriving at Aldershot. Euphoria over recent allied victories which had driven the Italians from North Africa and Abyssinia made the young trainees wonder if the war would be over before they could take part, but the picture soon darkened again. In April, Greece surrendered to the Germans and Rommel landed in force in Africa. In May the Luftwaffe destroyed the House of Commons.

The training at Aldershot acquired greater urgency. For Jack, one of the most rewarding elements was a wet-bridging course at Wouldham on the Medway, where they built 'floating bridges, especially the new Bailey pontoon bridge, and generally played about with motor boats and outboard motors'. He felt he was actually learning things which would be of practical use at the front. Despite the hard mental and physical labour, he had energy to spare:

We had two naval, twelve-oar cutters, each oar worked by two rowers. After a hard day's work I usually managed a place in the cutter race, always two or three miles up stream to the Five Bells. After a drink we would return more leisurely with the stream…

In October Jack was commissioned in the Royal Engineers and 'fitted up (at my expense) with a gorgeous uniform with brass buttons, a shining Sam Browne belt and a most fetching, I thought, dark blue fore-and-aft cap with regimental badge'. After a week's leave, he arrived in Clitheroe, where the battalion was housed in an old cotton mill. As would happen to him many times on the other side of the world, he was expected to master an entirely new situation with little or no support from his superiors. He was nineteen years old and he was to take charge of a training section.

The idea of being father confessor to 120 men, mostly tradesmen in their late twenties from north British industrial towns, was nothing short of horrific. Even worse, still green from OCTU, to be over regular NCOs with years of field experience. My company commander, a First World War dug out, was little help, being singularly economical in advice though more than extravagant in criticism. I soon lost count of the times that he threatened to have me court-martialled.

*However I had a great deal of luck. I was not looking
forward to my lecture on water supply in the field and
in my innocence I started, 'In the field only the medical
officer is allowed to pass water.' For a moment I wished
that the floor would open up beneath me but I soon
realised that they thought that it was a prepared joke
and laughed, making me a lot more confident. The
second 'luck' was quite extraordinary. I was to lecture
on explosives and decided to collect some samples from
the store. When we arrived at the store my sergeant
and I both thought that the other had the Yale key. On
impulse, I picked up a small piece of wire, put it into
the key slot and gave a twist and the lock sprung open.
After this incident I was treated with more respect. I
felt that some of my men were saying something like
'That officer of ours may look like a baby but he seems
to know a thing or two.' That night I went back to the
store and tried to repeat the miracle for twenty minutes
with no result.*

He found the Lancastrians generous and hospitable (though
the substitution of liquid paraffin for cooking fat had its
disturbing moments) and the months passed reasonably
enough. Administrative and pastoral responsibilities took
up much of the time left over from training and joint
exercises with the Home Guard, but there was the fun
of learning to ride a motorbike cross-country—and there
was Norah. Norah was a former nurse, now working in

her father's munitions factory. Jack met her by mistake while trying to contact another girl and promptly fell in love. When time off and the Ribblesdale bus schedules coincided, they would go dancing at the Empress in Burnley or walk on the moors above Clitheroe, dropping in at the Moor Cock for a drink. These snatched meetings were Jack's one consolation in his increasing impatience to be posted overseas.

A few months into the training, he was given the task of demonstrating bridging to local infantry units. A kapok assault bridge was to be thrown across the Ribble, followed by a folding boat-bridge which would take light tanks. As so often with his army experiences, events had a way of turning into pure comedy.

By the time the demo started, my job was finished (bar emergencies, the Sergeant was in charge). So, to add a bit of realism, I acquired a few primers and threw them into the river to simulate shell fire, sending up great plumes of water. Unfortunately, they also stunned a number of salmon which floated to the surface. Since I had trained my men well in resourcefulness, naturally those that floated past the bridge were hastily scooped up. At the end of the day we had a bag of eight or nine fine fish which were brought to me for dividing out among the various messes... One of the groups decided they did not like salmon and took their fish to the local fishmonger and the news somehow reached the water bailiff. There was a war on (in fact, so serious was the invasion threat that only a short time before we had handed in all our bayonets, to be mounted on scout staves and given over to the Home Guard). Nevertheless, a crime had been committed, the law ground into action and the criminal, Lt J Cripps, RE, who was in charge and therefore responsible, had to appear before the magistrates who duly found him guilty of poaching and fined him £3 (about a week's pay). On the evening of the court, I as usual called into the section's barrack room where Sergeant Hill saluted smartly and presented me with a cap full of pennies, threepenny bits and sixpences to the exact sum of £3. I felt my criminal record had been worthwhile.

Apart from the sadness of parting with Norah, it was a great relief to Jack to be posted at last in September 1942 to a field company at Wilsic Hall near Doncaster. One major assignment was to prepare local bridges for demolition in the event of a German landing. Watertight containers were needed for the explosive, which was only available in powder form. In a pre-plastic era this was a problem— until someone had the bright idea of using condoms. Jack was despatched into Doncaster to buy a hundred. Much too embarrassed to mention it to a female, he wandered disconsolately from chemist shop to chemist shop, acquiring quantities of toothbrushes and shaving soap, until he finally found a male assistant.

The stay at Wilsic Hall was enjoyable but brief. While his senior officers were away on a course and he was acting CO, a signal came through: an officer from the unit was to be posted immediately for service overseas. Jack seized the opportunity. 'As I was the only one with the rank and experience required and it seemed probable it was for service in the Western Desert, I posted myself and sent off the necessary documents.'

After a fortnight's embarkation leave in London, he reported to the RE Transit Depot in Halifax. There he was given tropical kit and a billet but no indication of where or when they would be going. The only hint came from their landlady, who denied all knowledge but casually mentioned that she had been told to change the sheets on a particular day. 'Well, the day we found clean sheets we packed extra carefully and, sure enough, that evening we marched down to the station to board a train.'

Their journey to the port lasted twenty-four hours, the blinds tightly shut all the way, and they boarded their ship in darkness. Jack had no idea of their eventual destination, nor how long it would be before he returned to England. What he did have was an eager resourcefulness, an intense interest in the world about him and an appetite for adventure. He was twenty years old.

Chapter One

Under cover of darkness, we boarded SS Largs Bay at Avonmouth and, in darkness and a thick fog, slipped out on the tide. By morning we were sailing north, still in fog, but towards evening it lifted momentarily to reveal a hazy glimpse of Rathlin Island and the great cliff of Fairhead on the Antrim coast. It was the last I was to see of the UK for nearly four years.

The fog persisted for four days, during which time we seemed to be going roughly north-west, though we never held any course for long, sailing instead in a series of zigzags in order to confuse any lurking sub-marines. On the fifth day, when we reached the deck for the daily roll-call, the fog had cleared. We were somewhere out in the cold and rough North Atlantic in convoy with five troopships, two or three merchantmen, an armed merchant cruiser, the Alcantara, and, most comfortingly of all, on each quarter the slim shape of a destroyer. It was a considerable feat of navigation since these ships had sailed from different ports all round Britain in thick fog and had met and taken up their convoy stations without the aid of radar, which was still in its infancy. We felt completely safe from anything the German navy could put against us.

I have always loved the sea or, perhaps more accurately, been fascinated by its mystery, its unpredictable and sudden changes of mood, from oily calm to raging storm and battering waves. Ever since man learned to build boats, the sea has thrown down the gauntlet of challenge to him. Contrary to all reason, he has accepted this challenge and pitted his mind, strength and skill against the might of storm and ocean. Over thousands of years, he has built stronger, safer and faster craft, with ever more sophisticated navigational aids, but even despite heroic feats of courage and endurance, he can never be sure of victory. Somehow, it seemed to be the sea our little convoy was battling against, and the very real danger from U-boats, mines and pocket battleships was almost unimportant by comparison.

The Largs Bay* was about 15,000 tons and in peacetime plied between the UK and New Zealand, taking passengers and cargo, especially chilled meat. Officers occupied the passenger cabins, which were refitted with three tiers of bunks. Hence there were three or six in a one- or two-berth cabin, with just standing-room in between. We ate extremely well in the old first class dining room; many of the pre-war kitchen staff were still there and there was a well-stocked bar. The original tables and chairs were replaced by long tables and built-in benches and we had two sittings.

Conditions for the men were radically different. They lived, slept and ate in the old cargo holds

*Her sister ship, the Jervis Bay, was converted into an armed merchant cruiser with strengthened decks and fitted with six-inch guns. In November 1941 she was on convoy protection duty when attacked by the German pocket battleship, Admiral Scheer. Although hopelessly out-gunned, she kept up the fight until all but five of the 38 ships in her care had scattered into the fog. She was last seen ablaze from stem to stern, with her guns still firing. (JHHC)

which had been fitted with long tables and back-to-back built-in benches, only leaving a narrow corridor in the centre. When all the benches were occupied by sitting men, the hold was considered to be full. At night some slept on the floor, some on benches, some on the tables. A few were able to sling hammocks. They did have some wash-places and loos, and a little deck space. In a dead calm it was horribly overcrowded, to say the least, but indescribable in an Atlantic gale—and we were on the sea for two months, with more than our share of rough weather. I never ceased to be amazed how they, mostly young men from all walks of life, or perhaps almost straight from school, managed to come on the daily parade on deck looking clean, tidy and reasonably cheerful. The human race is incredibly resilient.

Back to the officers: we were in comparative comfort, if a little cramped; it was always possible to find somewhere to sit and we had some deck space for exercise. As always, I was happy to spend hours just watching the changing moods of the sea and the other ships in the convoy. In really rough weather, our four destroyers ploughed right through the huge waves, emerging unscathed on the other side. Occasionally they would leave their stations and dash through the convoy, whether for training or for real, we never knew, once only clearing our bow by yards. Ships were always flashing signals in Morse, so I joined the Morse class but, though I got reasonably proficient with the buzzer, I could never transpose the light signals fast enough to read.

We had daily lectures on military subjects. I gave a few on explosives, mines and booby traps. I was also in an anti-aircraft team, though we secretly thought that our particular weapon was likely to be more deadly to the firers than to any enemy. Basically, it consisted of a battery of 'Guy Fawkes' rockets, which were attached to long pieces of wire. The theory was that when a dive bomber was spotted, you lit as many rockets as possible and the wires wrapped round the enemy propellers or even, hopefully, cut off a bit of wing. Actually, since there were no German aircraft-carriers at sea and we kept well away from land, they were unlikely to be used. Still, it was perhaps psychologically wise for us to have something to do in an emergency.

In the evenings, four of us usually found a corner to play bridge—never for anything but minimum stakes but as I usually played with the same partner we got to know each other rather well, so seldom lost over an evening.

Occasionally, I would make an unauthorised trip down to the engine rooms by one of the several escape hatches. Once down there, no one seemed to bother about me, though I did once have a bit of a scare. I went aft along a low and narrow passage that gave access to the propeller shaft. I was right in the stern, inspecting a leak in the very end of the shaft and engaging in an interesting speculation as to how long it would take to flood the ship if the pump failed, when an alarm bell rang. The watertight door closed inexorably behind me, cutting me off completely from the rest of the ship. The prospect of being trapped was very far from pleasant but natural optimism persuaded me not to panic (well, perhaps only a little) since surely there must be an escape ladder from this potentially watery tomb. After what seemed an age, another bell rang and the door slid slowly open again. I returned to the main part of the engine room with no delay and much relief.

Chapter Two

Convoys had to be refuelled en route for the Cape. Generally they did so in Freetown, on the West African coast, but we had heard rumours that we were bound for Brazil. So, after six weeks at sea, it was no great surprise to see land to our west and, later in the day, to find that we had dropped anchor in Bahia (now Salvador) harbour. This is not as odd as it at first seems. Wartime convoys kept well clear of any coast, as the Germans had a fairly extensive spy network which could alert the submarine packs, and a quick look at a globe will show that it is not much further to make a great sweep across the Atlantic instead of coming right into Freetown. In addition, Brazil had just joined the Allies and perhaps it made political sense, as well as taking a sea route unexpected by the enemy.

The dock facilities only allowed two ships at a time to be refuelled, so we remained in the middle of the harbour for the next two days—though not without some entertainment. After six weeks on a single-sex ship, even the distant view of a dusky maiden was an excitement and as the possessor of a pair of binoculars I was very popular. There was also an American tramp anchored alongside, with a boatswain who seemed to be perpetually inebriated, in which state he gave a continuous, dramatic and detailed oration about the qualities of the girls in the various ports. The best were without doubt in Rio, possessing the greatest staying power.

We had a rather disastrous lifeboat drill. Our lifeboats were wooden, clinker-built, of considerable age and fitted with a sail. Having paraded on our boat decks, we proceeded in an orderly way down a landing gangway and climbed into the boats, which were brought alongside by the crew and pushed off when full. Volunteers manned the oars and a crew member hoisted the sail. Off we set in a light breeze in the warm tropical harbour for a real treat after nearly two months cooped up in the ship. The sail had just started to fill when it became apparent that so had the boat—and very fast. With all hands to the oars, we made the landing gangway with only inches of free-board left. It appeared that most of the lifeboats were in a similar condition but for the rest of our voyage we did get a little comfort from seeing that they were hosed down regularly to plim the old dry wood.

Next morning we moored alongside the jetty, taking on fuel and fresh water, and after breakfast paraded and formed up by units on the jetty. The idea, we were told, was to march through the town, come back for lunch and then get shore leave. The march was not without difficulty. We were roughly in the middle of the column, equidistant between two Brazilian bands, both playing in (different) rhythms much more suited to South American dances than to marching. Under the circumstances, it was hard to give the impression of a smart, efficient British Army on the way to war. There were also other dis-tractions. This was obviously a great local occasion and the whole route was lined two or three deep with people of all ages. Many of the local belles had got into the front row and proclaimed their profession in unmistakable international language, doing their best to pass addresses to any likely-looking customers.

It was a glorious hot tropical morning, the road from the harbour climbed steeply into the town and we were unfit from our two-month confinement, so it was a great relief to stop after the regulation fifty minutes for a ten-minute break. By luck, we fell out outside the English-speaking club whose members brought us out pints of chilled beer, plus invitations to spend the evening in their homes. After two pints of beer, the return march felt distinctly as if Bahia was floating on a choppy sea. Back on ship, we went down for lunch, looking forward to our shore leave, only to find when we returned to the deck that the ship was once again in the middle of the harbour. In retrospect, it was probably a wise move: several thousand young men, average age about twenty, would have been like lambs to the slaughter in such a town after so long at sea.

One more day in the harbour and we put out again into the South Atlantic, where we soon ran into enormous seas. To describe the waves as large was an understatement; moving mountains of water was more descriptive. The Largs Bay was never for a moment still, climbing to the top of the waves before crashing down into the great foam-filled valleys, leaving the shuddering propellers, together with our stomachs, in limbo. After a week of this, I at last succumbed to seasickness.

Another two weeks and we awoke in a dead calm, with our engines just turning over. A trip on deck revealed a glorious clear summer day and an oily calm sea, with just a suspicion of gentle swell; away to the north was the unmistakable profile of Table Mountain. But what was so different was that the whole convoy was stationary, just holding against the current that slowly drifted past, carrying a grim flotsam

of wreckage. A ship, not in our convoy, had hit a mine and we had heaved to, waiting for minesweepers from Cape Town. We would have presented an irresistible target to any sub within miles. Air cover, even if available, certainly wasn't evident. It was a relief when a little flotilla of minesweepers arrived and we were once more slowly under way with paravanes fitted. In four days we sailed into Durban, welcomed in by the famous lady singing on the end of the jetty.

We disembarked in marching order with tin hats and battledress—which at the time seemed ridiculous but was made up for later—and went by train to a transit camp several miles out of Durban. We found ourselves (a batch of twelve officers) about half-way down the long reception queue. We were longing to get settled in and, hopefully, have a pass into town, so we weren't exactly pleased when, only a few feet from reception, our OC called us out of the line and talked a lot of nonsense. When he had finished, we returned to the very end of the queue and could gladly have murdered him. As we at last reached the front, a sergeant reported that the camp was full. We had an even longer wait, which did not in any way lessen our murderous feelings. Then, after a lot of telephoning, we were loaded into a truck and returned to Durban, to be put up in a luxury hotel right on the seafront. Murderous tendencies evaporated.

By some administrative error, all our kit except what we stood up in (battledress and tin hats, hardly suitable for the height of South African summer) had been put on a train to Johannesburg. The solution was obvious: a quick shopping expedition, and we soon supplied ourselves with suitable summer wear plus a bathing suit. Though we were supposed to be present at the three main meals of the day, we arranged for one of us to be present at each meal, with instructions as to where to contact the others, and Dave, John and I, who had become friends on the boat, set out for the beach.

There was no doubt that we were just off a troopship: our lily-white skins contrasted with the lovely bronzed bodies of the locals. After a delicious swim and a brief reconnaissance, we found ourselves chatting up three rather nice-looking young ladies. After a long time at sea, a bit of masculine showing off is natural and perhaps excusable. *Show Off 1:* despite plenty of warning about the near tropical sun, we took the line that if all these South Africans could take it, so could we. *Show Off 2:* there was a wreck about 400 yards from the shore, with a large notice emphasising the unsafeness of swimming to it. Well, Dave and I were strong swimmers, we would show them what the British were like. Hardly had we entered the water than we were on the wreck, waving to our new girlfriends. We dived off to return and soon realised that we were making no progress towards the shore but were being carried fast along the coast. Dave was a born philosopher and calmly theorised that if we simply kept afloat and swam gently shorewards we would come in somewhere along the bay. We did just this but only regained the beach half a mile away, after which we trotted back to our party with a masterly display of phlegm.

Naturally, we tried to date the girls for the evening but they were frustratingly unwilling to be committed and would only say that they'd return to the beach after lunch. In the afternoon they brought Mother along, putting us on our very best behaviour. Mother decided that we wouldn't be too bad an influence on her girls and asked us to dinner at her home.

After the drab, cold wartime English winter and months cooped up at sea, the next week was heaven.

We were in a land of warmth, colour and plenty, with unstinted hospitality and the company of three very lovely girls. We had a permanent evening invitation to their home and I persuaded Ann, who worked in Durban, to lunch with me. Several evenings we took them out to what must be the most romantic dinner-dance in the world. A path led from the restaurant down a flight of dimly-lit steps to a little marble dance floor, open to the stars and surrounded by the jungle. A concealed band played soft romantic music that couldn't quite drown the natural orchestra of cicadas and frogs, and a warm gentle breeze carried the heady scent of syringa and orange blossom.

Heaven it was, but we knew it couldn't last and indeed we didn't really want it to. We were not yet ready for heaven: we had been trained to fight for our country and wanted to get on with it. There was something else too. A week in the African summer sun was turning our English winter backs into a bit of physical hell. I had no idea there were so many layers of skin that could peel off.

Apartheid was not yet an official Government policy but there was little mixing of races, and justice for the non-whites was rather rough. One evening we were with our hostess family when an Indian and an African youth came into the compound fighting. In answer to a telephone call, a white policeman arrived, who enlisted the African's help to hold down the Indian while he was whipped, after which the Indian held down the African for the same punishment. Short and swift maybe, but not very aesthetic.

On the eighth day, our kit having returned from Johannesburg, we reported back to the transit camp and soon were on board another troopship. This time it was a smaller cargo ship with little cabin space, so we were in a hold, sleeping where we could. I opted for a hammock. Except for a horrific back, it wasn't too bad a journey as it was relatively short and calm and my bridge partner was still on board. Perhaps it would have been better not to have known that eight ships had been sunk in the Mozambique channel the previous week.

After eight days, shortly before Christmas 1942, we steamed safely into Mombasa harbour. We were expecting it to be just a refuelling stop but soon learned that here we were to stay.

Chapter Three

Strange indeed is the human mind. I was not in the least pleased or excited to find myself in this fascinating, beautiful country and to learn that it was to be my home for the immediate future. Quite the contrary: I was annoyed and disappointed for I had set my heart on joining a front-line unit in the Middle East. This could only mean more training and many months before I could get to the real war. Besides, I had no knowledge of Africans and not the least desire to work with them. As for the white settlers, I assumed they were all part of Kenya's infamous Happy Valley crowd.

Gradually the mysterious lure of Africa and its captivating people began to work on me and I began to understand, with Laurens Van der Post, that once you have lived in Africa, part of you will always remain there and become part of the great rhythm of African life. I also soon found that the Happy Valley was not representative of the great majority of white settlers. In retrospect, it was an experience I would not have missed for all the world.

Soon after disembarking, we were bound for Nairobi on East African Railways, in itself quite an event. The line is narrow-gauge, allowing it to turn through very tight curves, and the gradients are often so steep that the locomotives have to be huge and heavy. At this time they were still wood-burning and were never fast, with minimum acceleration, taking minutes to reach even a walking pace. No seasoned traveller ever boarded the train until well after the whistle, and would certainly not leave a drink unfinished if in the bar. Going up the great escarpments, many of the passengers would get off and walk. When the train stopped at a station, a queue carrying teapots formed by the engine and, on request, the driver would pull a lever that released jets of boiling water.

We spent a day in Nairobi, then only quite a small town with a couple of hotels and a dozen or so Indian-owned shops. (Shopkeepers and artisans were almost exclusively Indians, descendants of those who came over to build and work the railways.) Next morning, the Royal Engineers batch went on by train to Nanyuki, a small town on the equator but, at 6,000 feet, with a perfect climate. By day it was as hot as an ideal (but seldom met) English summer, while at night it was cool enough to make a wood fire welcome. It consisted of one wide street, a bank and three Indian-owned shops with corrugated iron roofs, remarkably reminiscent of a western film set.

It was still not our final destination. After another ten miles by truck, we came to where the Northern Frontier road met the great cedar forest that surrounded Mount Kenya. Except for patches of bamboo and a few clearings, the forest ran right up to the top of the tree-line, where it dissolved into a heath of extraordinary giant lobelia and groundsel and a multitude of tiny dwarf flowers, with the great glacier-covered peaks of the mountain beyond. A few days later, I found myself in what must have been the world's most perfect site for a camp. It was at about 6,500 feet, at the edge of the cedar forest which sloped gently up. The dense bamboo was interspersed with areas of open grassland full of zebra, wildebeest, buffalo, antelope and (heard more often than seen) hyena and lion and (definitely to be avoided) the black rhino. The camp itself was a natural amphitheatre enclosing a flat area big enough for a parade ground or football pitch. The lovely trees gave shade from the tropical sun and were occasionally the habitat for the beautiful black-and-white colobus monkey. A hundred yards away, a clean and lively stream provided all the water we needed. Fourteen miles to the east and 10,000 feet above were the snow-capped peaks of Mount Kenya.

For the next nine months we lived with the mountain towering above us, looking only a few hours' walk away, sometimes sparkling clear, dressed in virgin snow, sometimes shyly veiled in cloud but always mysterious and alluring. On a clear day, looking south across the savannah, one could just make out the white dome of Mount Kilimanjaro above the heat haze.

The camp came to be known as Ten Mile Camp and it was here that I met Dahir Abdul. On arrival, I was shown a round grass hut, with an African askari outside, and was told that for the foreseeable future this was to be my hut and this my personal orderly. The hut looked welcoming but, remembering what I had read about Africa, I looked (in vain) for the snakes, scorpions and tarantulas.

It was difficult to know what to make of Dahir. I had no experience of Africans and spoke only one word of Swahili, *Jambo*, and he had no English. We exchanged our one common word and a handshake and I was greeted by an impish grin. Dahir was quite unlike the rather large and dim black servant of children's books when I was young: he was medium height, slim but obviously strong and wiry, intelligent and very black. In my imagination I could picture him in the rigging of a Barbary coast pirate ship with a knife between his teeth. This was my introduction to a young man who was to become a very real friend, despite the fact that we were separated by language, culture, education, race and rank.

The forest had been cleared sufficiently for our party of five RE officers, twelve British NCOs and a handful of African domestic staff. Our orders, simple but hair-raisingly daunting, were to be ready in three days' time to take charge of upwards of 800 African askaris, mostly raw recruits, and train them to be combat engineers. Few, if any, would have any English, so we were to learn Kiswahili p.d.q. But first we were to Build Ourselves A Camp. This seemed just up my street. With the help of the Royal Engineers Pocket Book (1936), I got to work making out a formidable list of timber, nails, screws, doors, windows and corrugated iron that we would need for the first phase. On presenting the list at the CRE's office, we were told unequivocally that none of these things was available. There were, however, plenty of trees and grass for thatch, 'so get on and build yourself a camp'. We did get an issue of picks, shovels, axes and pangas.

With considerable apprehension we waited for our askaris to arrive. The apprehension was vastly justified. We had one clerk who spoke fairly good English and there were a few African NCOs who had at least some primary training, including an immensely tall Nubian sergeant-major. He, like most Nubians, was a dark ebony black but had virtually no English. My greatest shock was seeing my section on parade for the first time: a hundred superbly fit and tough-looking black men, all looking exactly the same. (Four years later, when I returned to the UK, I looked with dismay on a section of British recruits. Apart from a few Jamaicans, they were a uniform shade of white with no helpful tribal marks or tribal features.) The list of names was useless, being quite unpronounceable. However do you address and welcome your men with no means of communication? Between us, we had a very great deal to learn.

One of the first problems was the security of our tools. As yet we had no huts, so a guard was arranged, armed with a pick-helve and instructions, translated by the clerk as follows:

'If anyone approaches, say, "Halt, who goes there?" If they come on, repeat this, and if they still come on, count up to three and then hit them over the head with the pick-helve.'

The British quartermaster-sergeant decided, after dark, that he wished to check something. As he approached the store, out of the darkness came a deep voice.

'*Alti ugo ter?*'

'Don't be a fool, it's only me.'

'*Alti ugo ter?*'

'Come on, it's only me.'

'*Moja, Mbili …*'

At this stage the sergeant decided that a rapid retreat was the most sensible course of action.

The site for our camp was ideal, open to the south-west, but merging into the cedar forest on the other three sides. The forest had areas of dense undergrowth, interspersed with patches of rough grass, and was riddled with game tracks. Mostly the game kept out of sight, though occasionally you would surprise a dik-dik in the early morning or, less often, see colobus monkeys in the trees, and always there were plenty of exotic birds and butterflies. At night, the sounds of the forest were often creepily close. A pair of tree hyrax kept up a continuous call. We described them as the gramophone beasts, as they would call to each other, getting gradually quieter and slower, just like an old clockwork gramophone as it ran down… and then quite suddenly start up again in full voice. We also heard lions roar and, always sounding uncomfortably close, the laugh of the hyena—a particularly hair-raising noise.

There was certainly no shortage of building material. For the uprights and main trusses, trees were cut and split; for the roofs, there was wrist-thick bamboo less than a mile away and ample grass for thatch. Small round huts for the officers and British NCOs were no problem and the Africans built them to their own design. Each beam, according to its position and angle, had a different Swahili name. For messes and African sleeping quarters, we decided on oblong huts which, strangely, the Africans found very much more difficult, so we had to design and carefully supervise their building. We did, in fact, make the mistake of not giving enough pitch to the thatched roofs (on which the RE Pocket Book gave no guidance), resulting in considerable leaks at the first rains.

Meanwhile, training continued: basic marching, square drill and rifle drill, leading on to fieldcraft.

This caused endless difficulty, not only with the language but also the 'logic'. There is no exact Swahili equivalent of 'yes' and 'no'. The nearest is *ndio* and *hapana*, which are best translated as 'it is so' and 'it is not so'. For example, if you asked, 'Can you not find the axe?' the answer *hapana* (no) would mean 'What you say is not so.' Or, in English, 'Yes I have found it.' In a fieldcraft exercise, if I wanted an askari to take up a position beyond a certain tree, I would say, in English, 'Go behind that tree,' but in Swahili logic, since I am speaking and facing the tree, behind is obviously on my side of the tree, so *Mbele ya mti* (literally, 'in front of the tree') would be correct. At first, this led to considerable frustration and confusion to both races but in time the African way seemed easier and more sensible, to such an extent that half a century later I am sometimes not sure in which logic I am actually thinking. Time was also a problem: the army favoured the twenty-four hour clock, while to the African the day, starting at sunrise, was zero to twelve hours, and the night the same, thus leaving us with three separate time systems.

They were a happy, very lovable people but a people who, even after four years, would still hold plenty of surprises for me. We were given no official help in getting to know them. Even a one-day course would have saved months of frustration. As it was, most of us went through the same sort of progression. At first we treated them as perhaps rather thick English recruits, with rather poor results. Then we tended to adopt the worst kind of settler attitude, trying to bully them into submission. This was even less successful. At last, as we started to speak their language and to know a little of their culture, we realised that their outlook and philosophy were different from ours, in some ways actually superior, and we began to treat them on their own terms.

Most of our askaris came straight from tribal life and were almost untouched by western civilisation. For many, their journey to the training unit was the first time they had travelled in any sort of vehicle. Their tribal background was both good and bad: good in that the unit could be considered to be the tribe and they were proud to belong to it; on the other hand, an African sergeant would always recommend his own tribesmen for promotion and there were some tribal disputes. The British officers were, as it were, *in loco parentis* as the chief and had therefore to hold the askaris' respect, which was sometimes quite demanding. My personal orderly, Dahir, a gorgeous rogue, once said to me in Kiswahili, 'You are fighting for your flag. We don't understand that. I happen to like and respect you and will fight with you and die with you if necessary, but if I didn't I would just as soon cut your throat.' A very sobering thought.

Chapter Four

Our rations at Ten Mile Camp were good, except for a shortage of fresh meat and vegetables. Kenya's own brand of bully beef was also quite good—even if rumour had it that more camels and zebra than cattle entered the factory gates. Anyhow, to get to the point, I was made catering officer. I had heard that there was a farm only about a quarter of a mile from the camp and I set off to investigate.

I am not sure what I was expecting, but certainly the neat little bungalow in a garden bright with flowers was not my idea of a farmhouse. I knocked nervously on the front door and was completely thrown when it was opened by a large white lady with sufficient presence to be a duchess.

'I'm sorry, I, er, thought this was a farm.'

'Of course it's a farm.'

'I, er, was wanting some vegetables.'

'Of course you can have some.'

A businesslike contract for the supply of vegetables had just been drawn up when she suddenly asked, 'Do you ride?'

When I replied with an enthusiastic yes, she said, 'Thank God!' and invited me to come over and exercise her ponies next time I was free.

This was my introduction to Mu Bullock, who had farmed Narengenu since her husband died and her son joined the KAR. She felt that she ought to be in some way entertaining British servicemen but so far had found little of common interest since most of the British were townsmen and scared stiff of horses.

Next weekend I took up her offer and once she had seen that I was a confident rider she gave me *carte blanche* to come any time I could. Like most of the East African ponies, hers were Arab-Somali cross, very surefooted and trained to go for long distances at a slow comfortable triple—therefore ideal for riding through the game tracks. One has to be careful on the equator as there is virtually no dusk: within minutes of sunset it is dark and unless there is a moon it is unsafe to ride. At first I stuck to weekends.

A few weeks later I met one of Mu's bitch's puppies, an English setter-dalmatian cross called Mick, and was captivated. Common sense argued strongly against a serving officer having a dog, but I was lonely and had not really found any kindred spirits. Also, Mu promised to give him a home if and when I left, and the East African Engineers were reasonably relaxed in formal discipline and didn't object to a junior officer having a perpetual shadow.

After a fairly strict training, Mick settled down quickly into my lifestyle. He was dalmatian in colouring but more setter in conformation, with a lovely feathered tail. He inherited character from both sides. From the dalmatian side, he had the old coaching dog habit of trotting along happily and apparently safely right behind the horse's heels, and he soon learned to walk at heel on command. From his paternal side, he would instinctively set in the presence of game.

One day, when we had ridden rather fast over open country, Mick was lagging behind and I stopped fortuitously by a fallen tree. When he caught up, I waited for him to recover his breath, whereupon he jumped on to the tree trunk and then straight into the saddle in front of me. The pony, no doubt descended from a long line of overburdened Somalis, took it calmly and we rode on. As I have said, the ponies seldom trotted and Mick was quite happy at a walk or a triple and jumped down when he was rested. From then on, if he was lagging, I would wait by a bank or tree stump and he would take the hint. Later, when I was issued with a motorbike, he also travelled sitting on the petrol tank.

Dahir, being a Muslim, made a great show of keeping clear of Mick, especially his nose, but when I was out at night he felt it his duty to guard my hut and I frequently returned to find him and Mick curled up cosily asleep together on my rush mat.

On one of my visits, Mu said that her niece was coming to stay and in due course I was asked to supper to meet Ann. This was the beginning of a marvellous time for me. I had already come to love Africa and my job and the askaris and the freedom of life with the great ancient forest all around and the mysterious mountain beyond. Now, I had a suntanned blonde of sweet sixteen for a companion. How could I help being a little in love with Ann, with Africa and its sunshine and teeming life, and with very life itself?

With Ann's arrival, I got myself excused morning PT. Instead, Dahir would appear soon after five at the door of my little round thatched hut with a steaming cup of tea and some shaving water. At twenty to six it would be cold and still pitch-dark as, by the light of the tropical stars, Mick and I trotted off towards Narengenu.

By the time I tapped on Ann's window, the stars were surrendering one by one to the first light of dawn and all were gone when I had saddled up the two ponies. It was still shivering cold as we rode towards the mountain—sometimes there was even a touch of ground frost above the camp—but gradually the peaks would wear a brighter and brighter halo and there would be a glorious sense of warmth as the sun rose above the mountain to bring another equatorial day. By now we would often be in an area of open grass, full of zebra, wildebeest or Thompson gazelle, and sometimes even buffalo or a very occasional rhino. Then, all too soon, back to the farm, where Ann would take over the ponies and I would return to the camp for breakfast.

On one of our morning rides, Ann and I surprised a recent recruit washing in a nearby stream. (The tribal Africans are very clean people. For instance, on troopships it was always the lack of washing facilities of which they complained, whereas I never heard British troops complaining about anything other than food.) The recruit was, of course, stark naked and, like most Africans, particularly well endowed in certain parts. He was in a quandary. Even at this early stage of training he knew that an officer should be saluted, but also that it was not etiquette to be so exposed before a girl and perhaps especially a white girl. His solution was ingenious and instantaneous. He leapt to his feet and, with a movement worthy of a belly dancer, swung and caught the offending organ between his legs and, only then, saluted smartly. To return the salute with a straight face was difficult.

Life was idyllic and yet I was impatient to get to the war, or at least to get on with training. The Africans were learning fast but we had virtually no engineering equipment. We knew we would be moved at some stage to a camp with water for bridging training but we had virtually no explosives either. Then I was offered about half a ton of gelignite. There was a disadvantage: old gelignite sometimes gets 'wet', when the nitro-glycerine oozes to the surface, and at this stage it is said that even a fly walking on it can detonate it. This batch was available because the process was just starting but I took the line that it would be safe to use for a week or so.

We made a pit in the ground, roofed it over with bamboo and thatch, and very carefully stowed the gelignite. For a few days we had some valuable practical explosive training. Trees were dramatically felled, large holes appeared in the ground and some old bits of scrap iron were neatly cut up. Then one afternoon a message came to say that a grass fire was sweeping towards Narengenu farm. I quickly collected about twenty men and we doubled down to the farm, only to find that Chris, Mu's son, was there and had saved the situation by control-burning the grass round the buildings. As we ambled back, it became clear that another fire was sweeping towards the camp and must be very near my explosive store.

Once more at the double, we approached the store to find that the fire had already caught the thatched roof. In my absence, my African sergeant Ayieko had taken command. The boxes of highly sensitive gelignite had been moved by a human chain and unceremoniously thrown on to a three-ton truck. At the very moment we arrived, it was just moving off with the last box on board. I felt my hair stand on end. I ordered the driver out and took over the wheel myself, driving it as though it was made of Venetian glass about a mile to an old quarry. We unloaded it with great care and then at a safe distance initiated an explosion, the like of which there could not have been since Mount Kenya ceased to be an active volcano.

Occasionally I would set out with some tracker askaris and a 303 army rifle with the point of the bullet sawn off (to give a dumdum spreading effect, causing almost instantaneous death at short range). I have never enjoyed killing anything but we were often short of fresh meat and I was a good shot with a rifle. By paying a small fee, I got a game licence entitling me to shoot one lion, I think, one rhino and quite a number of meat animals.

On one occasion we had been out on the plains for several hours and had shot enough for the camp (two antelopes, both killed instantaneously) when we met two South African Air Force trucks, each mounting a machine gun which had been used for shooting indiscriminately into herds of gazelle. Some of the Boer farmers seem to consider all grass-eating game to be vermin. After they had killed and collected two Thompson gazelle, they left several others wounded, probably to die slowly and painfully of wounds. It made me wonder why God had not destroyed the entire human race in the flood.

I would rather forget this next incident but honesty makes me include it. One day Mu told me that the zebra herds were getting out of hand on her grazing land and that she could also do with some zebra meat for her dogs. (Most Africans will not eat zebra meat, saying that it is bitter.) She lent me an Italian rifle with five rounds of ammunition. I believe that showing off before the opposite sex is a characteristic of the shy, rather repressed young man. If so, I was no exception, and Ann was there. Although a good shot, I did not know this gun and I should never have attempted my first shot at an outside range. Unfortunately, I didn't miss, but hit a zebra in the stomach. As I tried to approach it, it moved off. I tried two more shots at even greater range, to no effect. With only three rounds left, I couldn't afford any more and had to follow the poor wounded creature as it gradually grew weaker and weaker, leaving a thin trail of blood, till at last I caught up. The zebra looked round and I almost heard the words, 'Now finish me off, you bastard.' Thank God I was able to do this quickly with one shot. I felt like a murderer and could not have been far from putting the last round through my own head.

Some months after this we were again short of fresh meat, so Mick and I and two trackers set off into the forest. We kept finding fresh droppings but no game. The trackers blamed Mick, who had remained obediently at heel the whole time, and we decided to call it a day and return to the camp. I allowed Mick to take the lead. Suddenly he set, his head and tail in one straight line, and made a low, near inaudible growl. He was pointing at some thick undergrowth, through which I could see a greyish rump that I thought for a moment was an elephant. One of the askaris whispered, *'Mbogo mbaya sana'* (buffalo, very bad) and started to creep away. The other whispered, *'Nyama msuri sana, piga piga'* (very good meat, shoot, shoot).

I had vowed never again to shoot if I couldn't almost guarantee an instant kill, so I certainly could not shoot from where I was. The wind was coming towards us and it looked as if I could crawl slowly forwards until broadside on, but still protected by thick bush. I did just this and eventually found a gap through which I could get a perfect shot from only a few yards distant. I was very slowly working into a comfortable position for a steady heart-shot when something made me look over my right shoulder. There, not thirty yards away across a patch of open grass, was a massive bull buffalo.

I must have been terrified but my terror took the form, not of panic, but of complete inability to move. Instinctively I froze, looking across at this magnificent prototype of savage power. He lowered his monstrous five-foot spread of horn, at the same time sniffing the air and pawing the ground. I could clearly see the whites of his eyes. After what seemed an eternity, he gave a final contemptuous shake of his head and sauntered off. Instinct, probably acquired in this very continent millions of years ago, had saved me by causing such a pitiful display of weakness. We returned to the camp with no meat.

I had a standing invitation to supper at Narengenu once a week while Ann was staying and, naturally, greatly looked forward to it. One evening I arrived to be told by Mu, who never minced words, that Chris was home for one night only and my invitation was rescinded for the evening. To soften the blow, I was given a stiff drink but I returned to the mess in a distinctly bad mood just as the meal was starting.

British officers received a whisky allowance of about a quarter-bottle a month, while British NCOs had a ration of beer. (The Africans were only allowed to brew their native beer *pombe* by special permission of the CO and this was usually reserved for an occasional *ngoma*.) Of course, officers could also obtain various bottles from the Indian shops. My OC, a regular soldier, was a kind and generous man and, seeing my mood, said, 'Have a whisky, old boy?'

'Thank you.'

Blop-blop-blop-blop-blop-blop-blop.

'Water, old boy?'

'Please.'

Blip.

At this stage, the whisky ration ran out.

A few minutes later, 'Have a brandy, old boy?'

Blop-blop-blop, etc.

'Water?'

Blip.

By the second course, apparently, the brandy also was exhausted.

'Have a gin, old boy?'

Blop-blop, etc,

'Water?'

Blip.

The rest of the evening is a bit hazy but I do remember getting myself under enough control to wish my colleagues good night and with a great effort guiding myself to my hut.

There was an incident on the way. The direct route took me past the urinal. This was a masterpiece of construction by the company tinsmith, made from top- and bottomless ten-pound bully beef tins, four uprights and a top at forty-five degrees. For a quite unknown reason, this would not stay still. Swaying from side to side made it difficult to use but when I grasped it, it promptly collapsed.

Next morning my pillow and bed were in a ghastly mess and I felt equally ghastly for several days. Dahir

Abdul took it all completely in his stride but I vowed, *never again.*

Chapter Five

By day and night there was always a drumbeat to be heard. The drum played an important part in the tribal Africans' life and it became such a part of all our lives that generally, like the ticking of a clock, we ceased even to notice it.

Ann left Narengenu, only occasionally returning for short visits, and Africa and her people became more and more part of me and my thinking. I was an agnostic, certainly, but somehow, living here, it was not possible to believe that all this had happened without plan or planner. Our askaris came from many different tribes and as many faiths. We had

Anglicans, Roman Catholics, Methodists, Seventh Day Adventists, Mohammedans and others, and some were described as pagans but, to a man, they had a tremendous sense of 'at-oneness' with nature and equally an acceptance of what life brought. *Shauri ya Mungu* (literally, 'the affair of God') meant just this.

One of my fads was a dislike of tin mugs. I preserved my own china mug for three years of army life until Dahir one day brought me the pieces.

'Mungo alitoa mkona mangu.' ('God lifted it out of my hand.')

This was a simple and true statement of fact, so to contradict it and be angry would clearly be blasphemy.

Dahir was a follower of Islam but it seemed that his God only saw through human eyes. We had an issue of special bully beef for the Muslims, 'killed by a member of the faithful'. Once it failed to arrive and Dahir brought me a tin and asked if it was all right for him to eat. After reading the label, I said regretfully that it was not. A few minutes later he returned with an identical tin and again asked if it was OK, adding hastily, 'I can't read, you know.' I took the hint and said, 'Oh yes, this one is all right.' Despite the fact we both knew to the contrary, he ate it contentedly.

As age and arthritis creep on, one is more than grateful for the warmth and comforts of modern civilisation but it takes one further from the at-oneness of primitive Africa. This mystical revelation first came to me with stunning force on a night exercise at about 7,000 feet in the Mount Kenya forest. My section were resting, hoping to snatch a short sleep in a natural hollow at eye level, if one stood, with a great grass plain. It was dark except for the stars and all was quiet, except for omnipresent, mysterious whispers of the forest. The sentries listened intently for any sign of the 'enemy' somewhere in the forest searching for us. Then, a noise like distant thunder as a herd of wildebeest stampeded past, only a few feet from our heads. For a moment I was transported into a dimension out of time and was an integral part of Africa, part of African life and even of evolution itself. I have had the same entrancement alone on the bows of a ship ploughing through huge Atlantic seas and even sometimes when running on the springy turf of the English downs, when I felt as though suspended, weightless, as the grass rushed past my feet.

The training continued and the company, 72 Field Company EAE (and for me, especially, my section of about 120 men) began to cohere into a unit. There was one trouble. At home we had been able to reject up to about ten per cent of our recruits, after various aptitude tests, as unsuitable for the Royal Engineers. In Africa this was difficult, as no such tests had been devised and they were in theory all volunteers. In practice, the District Commissioners suggested to each chief that King George expected x 'volunteers' from his tribe and it was often a case of 'You, you and you'—and just occasionally, one suspected, some that the chief might have been quite glad to get rid of. If we could have done a 'Gideon' (Judges 7, 2-7) and kept the best eighty per cent, we would have had one of the best fighting units of all time.

Nevertheless, they were a great crowd and fun to be with. Many of the Luo tribe NCOs could not pronounce r and at the start of a march would shout out the time, 'Lefti liti, lefti liti', but soon they would break into song, individual askaris taking turns to sing the verses, ad lib, and all joining in the chorus. Many of the words were in tribal languages and often about their officers—I'm sure not disrespectful, by their standards, though some might have objected to having their personal lives sung about. I was *Bwana mrefu* (tall) or *Bwana kiko* and my rides with Ann had not gone unnoticed. (*Kiko* means pipe. We had a cigarette and pipe tobacco ration and, as I was the only pipe smoker among the Europeans, I had an unlimited ration and smoked a great deal too much.)

We had some detonators and primers and various bits of apparatus for making booby traps. Frequent Afro-European competitions in setting and defusing booby traps were always won by the Africans. We devised far more devious and sophisticated traps, but the Africans could always spot anything artificial.

One day I was asked to arrange a demonstration for local infantry officers and NCOs. All was carefully planned and an area, in which were hidden various small charges, cordoned off with white tape in front of my table. I was going to talk about explosives in general, then go on to booby traps, with practical demonstrations, and lastly cover minefield laying and clearing. The audience was duly seated on benches in the safe area and the lecture started. Quite disgracefully late, in my opinion, one brigadier arrived, advanced right into my danger zone and sat himself down on his shooting stick. I finished the explosives-in-general part. Now for the booby traps.

I gave the matter careful thought. I could not order a senior officer to retreat without explaining my plan, which would completely spoil the impact of surprise (paramount in military strategy). I reckoned that the brigadier was not in much physical danger, though some face might be lost, but then brigadiers should not be late. So the talk went on.

'Now, a booby trap consists of a lethal explosive that is detonated by some simple act as, for instance, picking up this book.'

As the book was picked up, there was a loud bang and the brigadier was temporarily obscured from sight by a cloud of dust. I sat down with an exaggerated expression of surprise and horror and poured myself a stiff drink.

'Or by, say, lifting a glass,' initiating another explosion. I am glad to say the brigadier had now retreated several yards and by the end of 'mine-laying and clearing' was at a very safe distance.

After about six months at Ten Mile Camp, we moved to a camp at the edge of Nanyuki, where we were on a small stream and had at least some bridging equipment. Most of the whites liked being closer to civilisation, such as it was, but for me PT was a poor substitute for my morning ride in the forest. However, I found an old chap who ran a riding school based alongside the nearby polo ground. I asked him if he would hire a pony at weekends. The answer was no, but he would give me riding lessons. After the first lesson, he told me that my riding was appalling but he didn't reckon he could teach me any more in a short time, so what about polo lessons? Why not? I thought. The war still seemed a long way off.

At first, I sat on a wooden horse at the centre of a bowl-shaped area with a wooden fence round the top, playing a kind of one-man DIY polo. When I hit the ball, it came whipping back from any direction, allowing me to try all sorts of shots with no danger to a live horse. When my instructor was satisfied, I graduated to the polo ground and a lovely old horse who must have taught generations to play. At first, he would walk up to the ball and stop dead until I hit it. Then he would walk up to the ball and, if I hit it, deign to trot, and so on until we might be at full gallop. But if I missed, it was back to a walk again and no nonsense—except on one occasion at full speed when he kicked it on with his back foot. (I do accept that this may have been chance!)

On Saturday afternoons, the local settlers would meet at the polo ground with their ordinary working ponies. If eight turned up, then a game was arranged. For several Saturdays I played on my hired pony.

This was polo at its best. Anyone who could really handle a pony was welcome, and the ponies were of much the same standard. It is quite the most thrilling game that I have played. I am not a good ball-game player but control of the pony is nine tenths of polo and I already had the advantage of having ridden my father's superbly trained Butterball in India. Of course, these ponies were not well trained but still seemed to enter the spirit of the game. There must be some telepathy between man and beast or how else was it that, without spurs or stick and only one hand for the reins, the pony would suddenly be going full gallop to exactly where you intended and then, as suddenly, following the ball in the opposite direction?

Then, one day, Mr Rimington announced that he was leaving Nanyuki, ponies and all. By now I was hooked, so next Saturday I arrived at the ground, trying to look like a seasoned polo player. This was a little difficult as I had no breeches but wore my army trousers with a leather strap below the knees (made to my design by the Nanyuki cobbler). My luck was in. Only seven players turned up. A complete stranger approached me, asking if I played, and offered me his second pony. I must have passed the test as, after the game, Captain Adsley told me that although he lived in Nanyuki he was in the KAR. He was leaving the district but would send his *sais* down with the ponies every Saturday, or any other time I liked. Unfortunately, I too left a few weeks later.

Anyone who knows the working of the military will not be surprised that, because of my name (Sir Stafford Cripps had been the great poor man's advocate), I was frequently selected to take part in courts martial. This had started in the UK, where I became reasonably well versed in the Army Act and King's Regulations, and continued in Kenya. While in the Nanyuki camp, I was acting as defending officer for an African. The court, a Nissen hut, was a mile away and I was driven there, leaving my dog Mick in the camp. The case was not finished by lunchtime and was adjourned for an hour. I walked back to the

Nanyuki Club (serving officers were honorary members) for something to eat and, as I entered, a very pleased Mick came out from under a bar stool with an 'I knew I'd find you here' expression. Of course, he followed me back to the court and was instructed to sit outside.

The court continued.

Defending Officer: 'I will now call the first witness for the defence, Njani Iako.'

The door opened and in trotted a very cock-a-hoop dog, who was quickly ejected by the court orderly.

The second witness for the defence was announced. Mick tried again but was unceremoniously thrown out. A minute later there was a noise behind me and a head and shoulders wriggled through the open window, followed by a body and fluffy tail, and sat itself down quietly under my table.

President of the Court (a brigadier): 'I think there will be less disturbance if the Defending Officer's dog is allowed to remain in court.'

A certain nuance in his voice made me suspect that he was a dog lover.

That day proved to be rather eventful. I again called in at the club on my way back to camp and met Mary, another settler's daughter, who told me that there was a dance on. Would I join her party? I accepted enthusiastically, especially as, after the court martial, I was already dressed in my best uniform. Presently Mary introduced me to an attractive, dark, vivacious girl called Delia.

As an opening remark, I said, 'The last girl I knew of your name was a dreadful creature at school with me at a ghastly place called St Neot's.' (Not really co-ed, but she was the headmaster's niece.)

'What a coincidence. I knew an awful boy called Jackie at the same school.'

Perhaps we had both improved.

In due course, I paid a visit to the outside 'gents'. As I stepped out of the club door, a sinister figure leapt at me from the shadows. Unarmed combat (a form of karate) was part of army training but just in time, before I delivered a crippling kick in the lower stomach, I realised that it was Dahir. He gave me a thorough dressing-down for appearing at the club with filthy brass buttons and unpolished Sam Browne and shoes. I was stripped down to shirt, pants and socks. When I returned to the party, never before had my brass and leather so shone.

Sometimes I played a game of squash with Mary at the Nanyuki Club. Afterwards she often invited me back to the farm for supper, after which I would walk the five miles back to the camp. The rough dirt road went through both farmland and wild bush and when I was alone it was a bit creepy. There might well be wild animals about, though they were most unlikely to attack a human, but still every shadow could be a watching lion and every rustle a stealthy hyena. The protective presence of my beloved Mick made it infinitely creepier. In true setter style he would suddenly point at a bush, emitting a low growl. Unfortunately, as we didn't speak the same language, there was just no telling if he was on the scent of a mouse or a lion.

About this time, an engineer section was wanted to travel up to Abyssinia to instruct the other units in mine-laying and clearing. I felt my section was ideal, volunteered and was given the job. For some reason, it was also decided that the whole unit should have a general's inspection. This did not please me: I had a lot to do in getting my section ready to go, including a crash revision course in mines, while the OC wanted them to waste far too much time on square-bashing to polish up their drill. My tropical uniform was, I have to admit, on the worn side, but I would not agree with Dahir that I must get the Indian tailor to make me a new one, just for one general. Surprisingly, Dahir seemed to take it very stoically but a couple of days before the inspection it dawned on me that my askaris had taken a lot of trouble to smarten themselves up, whereas their officer would look like a scarecrow. However, when the day of the inspection came, there laid out on my bed was an immaculate, apparently brand new tropical uniform.

'Be careful with it, Bwana. I have borrowed it from the Bwana Colonel's boy in the next camp.'

Before setting off to Abyssinia, I was asked to a party at Delia's farm. It was a clear tropical night with a full moon and the chief diversion was a game of 'French and English', played on horseback (a game consisting of two sides, each attempting to take the other captive). There was a lot of open grazing land, ideal for this, and the porcupine holes had been filled in. I very nearly came off when my (borrowed) pony decided the dark mark of a track was a ditch and jumped it at full speed.

There was another pony incident when Ann, who was now running a riding school at Limuru, asked me to look at a pony she was hoping to buy. It was one of a batch coming down with a dealer from Somalia and was due to rest at Narengenu on the way. I think I was the first white man that it had ever met or—probably more relevant—smelt. (The Africans claimed that white men smelled foul, especially if they had eaten onions or cheese.) Anyhow, it took a great dislike to me and had me off three times in Mu's yard by the most vicious bucking I have ever felt. Fourth time lucky: I seemed to be in control and so took him off for a ride in the forest. All went well for ten minutes until I decided the girth needed tightening. As I put my leg forward and bent over to do this, I took off and so did the pony. Seconds later, I landed bottom first on a very hard tree stump. I still had the reins and bridle, but no pony. It was a long, painful stagger back to the farm, where the pony had long since arrived.

Chapter Six

At last we were ready to leave for Abyssinia. We set off with my two British sergeants, a British MT corporal, 120 Africans and Mick, together with a load of mines, booby-trap mechanisms, water drums and ample hard rations, all loaded on to twelve three-ton Chevrolet trucks. These were terrible. They had been salvaged from South African dumps, each truck being made up from the least bad bits of several wrecks, and that was just what they felt like to drive.

At first the road took us through the lovely 'White Highlands', with many prosperous-looking farms, sleek European cattle and fertile cornlands, before dropping down to the police post at Isiola. Dogs were not supposed to travel beyond here but Mick, who usually sat with me in the front, was buried under twenty odd askaris in the back and was not noticed. We were now in the hot dusty lava plain, which seemed to be void of any sort of life. Even the few scattered thorntrees looked dead. The dirt roads, never good, got even worse; the fine lava dust was all pervasive, turning blacks and whites into a uniform shade of dirty grey. I was spoilt, being in and usually driving the first truck but, even so, the dust was awful. With the state of our trucks and the roads, it was only possible to make about a hundred miles a day if we were to have time to set up camp, collect firewood and cook a meal.

We crossed the Juba near Bardera on a pontoon-raft characteristic of a Royal Engineer job. It ran across the river attached to a wire cable, taking two trucks at a time, and was driven solely by the flow of the stream, the pontoons being warped according to which direction one wanted to go.

We camped one night at Badoa (one of the worst famine areas in 1992) where I was entertained by the police officer. This had been Italian Somaliland and during the Italian period had been administered by a large military staff headed by a brigadier, but during the Allied occupation it was all in the charge of a single colonial police captain. He told me of the first case he had to judge, after which, unusually, there was an appeal. The defendant had been found guilty, which everyone knew he was, but since he had bribed every member of the jury and was *still* found guilty, this clearly could not be justice!

The water table at Badoa must have been falling for centuries and the wells had followed it down hundreds of feet. One long-dry well was used at the police house as a loo. It was intriguing to hear the results of your labours several seconds later from the bowels of the earth. (I heard years later that the loo superstructure was destroyed by an explosion of gas when a visitor, having dropped his keys, used a bit of lighted paper to investigate. He was apparently not seriously damaged.)

From here, the road took us to Mogadishu, one-time capital of Italian Somaliland. Mick had developed eczema, so I thought I would get him clipped in this prosperous and beautiful little town. I went to the HQ of the military administration to get advice and was put on to a red-headed Italian secretary. Unfortunately we had no language in common and I had left Mick in the camp but, after I had mimed a dog being clipped, she smiled and seemed to understand, writing an address down for me. I took Mick to the said address, only to find that Madame's establishment, though it had 'the most beautiful girls of every colour', had nothing to do with clipping dogs but everything to do with fleecing young men.

Having escaped inviolate, I repaired to a café to plan my next move. While eating an ice-cream, I noticed a poodle behind the counter which had obviously been clipped recently. With the help of the dogs and the proprietress's little English, I made myself clear this time. She produced the smallest pair of embroidery scissors, saying, 'I take one week, perhaps you quicker?'

I explained that I only had the rest of the day there and after a great deal of talking behind the counter she returned with the address of a Count Ceriani who 'had horses plenty'.

The count proved most unwilling to lend me his horse-clippers but we were lucky: his teenage daughter appeared. All the Italian officers having been sent to prisoner-of-war camps, she must have been a little bored and decided that I was the next best thing. She took a fancy to Mick (or me) and quickly and efficiently clipped him herself. The eczema improved almost overnight, but I was a little sorry that I had to leave Mogadishu the next day.

After Mogadishu we got on to the Strada Imperiale, one of the great Italian colonial roads, built quite straight, with cuttings and embankments and tarmac. We were most impressed as there were no motorways at home at this time and we had never seen anything like it. Despite our old trucks, we made nearly 500 miles in two days. Once across the border into British Somaliland, the roads reverted to dirt and dust.

At last we reached our destination, the town (hardly more than a village) of Hargeisia on the edge of the Ogaden desert. At this time it was in Abyssinia but is now part of Somalia. I reported to the brigade HQ for further orders, to find to my dismay that they knew nothing about me or what I was supposed to do. At any rate, we were allotted a site to set up camp and given some rolls of concertina barbed wire for security and, most importantly, put on the brigade ration strength.

The brigadier said, 'Well, since you are here, what would you like to do?'

After discussion it was decided that I should give a demonstration to the whole brigade and then run a course for officers and NCOs. The site was far from ideal, in the middle of an open, hot and dusty plain, bare of vegetation except for clumps of hard dry grass and a few thorny shrubs, and completely lacking protection from sun or wind. Around noon every day dust devils would sweep across the plain, drawing up great whirling spirals of dust capable of picking up almost anything in their path. Through the heat shimmer, you had a distant, tantalising view of greener, cooler hills.

At night you frequently heard the weird laugh of the hyena. He is a natural ventriloquist and somehow always makes his laugh sound as though he is just behind you. In Swahili this grotesque creature with its disproportionately massive shoulders, head and jaw is known as a *yangau*, a word they use to describe any large spanner or wrench.

The demonstration was going to employ every-one we could spare. Working with potentially lethal mines and explosives, it was easier for the askaris not to have to carry their rifles around, though we knew the Somalis were always hungry for any unguarded rifle. This caused a security problem. Our solution was to keep out six rifles for the guard and bury the rest under the guard tent. Unfortunately, as it turned out, I allowed the British NCOs to keep theirs in the guard tent by day and with them at night. As usual, I kept my revolver (loaded) on my belt by day, and at night under my pillow, attached by a lanyard to my wrist.

Training for the demonstration proceeded and the brigade signals sergeant came over to fix some amplification equipment. Metal detectors did exist but we

had none and would have to use dummies in the demonstration. I knew how they worked in theory and asked the sergeant if he could make one and fix it up to the Tannoy system. To our mutual surprise, it worked rather well but was enormous and quite impracticable to use in the field. However, when carried by our largest askari as far away as the wire would reach, it looked reasonable and made a satisfactory screech as it passed over a real mine.

The day came and, because there was very little happening in this remote area, it was considered a good day out for the military from far and wide. By zero hour the signal staff had at last got the Tannoy system to work and the cordoned-off area looked like the Silver Ring on Derby Day, bristling with loud-speakers and packed with all ranks. I knew I could rely on my NCOs and askaris but completely lacked confidence in myself.

'Gentlemen, a field section of 67 Field Company East African Engineers will now give a demonstration of laying and clearing a minefield.'

My nervous voice shouted back at me from six loudspeakers but, reassuringly, a party of askaris doubled smartly out and proceeded efficiently to lay mines, hardly giving me time to explain what they were doing. My confidence began to build up. At this moment the signal sergeant stuck his head out of his van and said, 'The f***ing system is f***ing well working at last.'

Replying in a language that he would understand, I said, 'Yes, it's all going f***ing well.' To my worse than horror, I was still holding the microphone switch and my words blared back at me. Panic! This was the end of my career. No officer or gentleman could use such language in a broadcast. Oh, that the ground would open up. Then I saw that the audience, to a man, was looking toward the nearest loudspeaker. I was just an unknown voice out of sight. I quickly pulled myself together and said, 'Sorry, gentlemen, a slight technical hitch.' After a short burst of laughter, the circus continued.

After a few days to reorganise, we started a six-day officers' course. I did rather well out of this. It was non-residential and news got around that I was to write a report on each officer at the end of the course, with the result that I received invitations to dinner at different officers' messes on the day their small drink ration arrived.

On the last day of the course, at about midday, I was in my tent marking the exam papers. Suddenly, there was a great roar as an especially large dust devil swept through the camp. It tore a huge rent in the top of my bell tent and sucked up all the papers. In a second it was all over and I could see the devil sweeping on across the plain, every now and then discharging bits of paper. I called out the guard, who chased the thief for miles across the plain, actually retrieving all but one of the exam papers. I was just a little suspicious of that missing paper as I was fairly sure its author had not taken the course as seriously as it deserved. Was he perhaps one of the devil's chasers?

That weekend was particularly hot and dusty and the allure of the hills was too much for me. I asked the NCOs if anyone would like to accompany me on a walk but no one was interested. I knew that there were bands of 'Shifter' about (wild, armed tribesmen dispossessed by the Italians) but I wasn't too worried and set off by myself. I suppose I had walked about four miles and was just beginning to climb the foot-hills, already a little less airless, when I noticed a sinister figure about half a mile behind me, carrying a rifle. When I stopped, he stopped. If I went on, so did he.

It was clearly time to think. Panic was prevented by the army training of rapid situation-assessment. Going on further into unknown country was not the answer. Could I make a dash for it? No, I might well twist an ankle on this rocky ground. I checked on my revolver. Yes, it was in the holster on my belt, and loaded. The closer we got, the more advantage lay with a revolver over a rifle. *Plan:* to turn round and walk back as nonchalantly as possible. The distance between us got less and less. I mustn't waste any of my six rounds, therefore I must let him make the first move and consequently lose the initiative. Then suddenly I realised it was Dahir.

'What on earth are you doing?'

'This is a very dangerous place, Bwana. I thought your mother would like to know where you died.'

'I couldn't stand that hot camp a moment longer.'

'Nor could I, Bwana.'

We decided that, with a rifle, a revolver and a dog, we were a match for any who came, so another about-turn. Together we spent a cooler evening wandering happily through the hills. (Only now, fifty years later, does it occur to me to ask how he got the rifle and ammunition, and on whose authority.)

A few nights later, I was woken around midnight by Mick barking furiously, which was most unusual. As I leapt out of bed, revolver in hand, he rushed through the triple concertina wire, still barking. Despite the starlight, I could see nothing. By now the NCOs had appeared to say that two of their three rifles had been stolen. We called out the guard and later the whole unit but, not surprisingly, searched in vain.

In the morning I looked at the place where Mick had been. Someone in bare feet had jumped the wire, presumably having thrown the rifles to an accomplice. More sinister, there under the wire between Mick's footprints was a vicious Somali dagger with a razor-sharp curved blade buried up to its hilt. I had a nasty nagging feeling that there just might have been inside information. Certainly, a night check quite often revealed very attractive Somali girls outside the camp wire. (The standard treatment was to deprive the poor girls of outer clothing and deport them several miles outside the town, *pour encourager les autres.*

It was definitely successful in reducing further visitations.) Wise after the event, we parked the trucks at night facing outwards, so within seconds the guard could illuminate the plain.

The loo for whites was about a hundred yards from the camp and was just a trench surrounded by an old bit of tent wall. Unfortunately, the tent wall kept disappearing during the night. The sergeants asked permission to fix up a booby trap one evening. Anticipating a small charge such as my 'brigadier-scarers', I gave permission. During the night there was an enormous bang from the loo area and on investigation we found a dead and mutilated hyena. To my horror, they had put quite a big charge in a piece of pipe. I never allowed it to be repeated but the message was taken and we lost no more tent walls.

Once or twice a week the NCOs went to the NCO club where they had a liberal ration of beer, denied to officers, so I always asked them to bring me back a bottle. This never happened until one night, when I was woken about midnight by all three NCOs coming into my tent, each with a pint bottle of beer.

'We couldn't take it away till it had been opened, so you will have to drink it now.'

Actually, it was a hot night and very welcome but I must have been a comic sight, sitting up in my camp bed, solemnly drinking three pints of beer with three NCOs looking on, while Mick, disturbed from his mat, sat stiffly at the end of the bed with a not-amused expression worthy of Queen Victoria.

Chapter Seven

I was rather pleased with my little 'circus'. We had done well what had been asked of us and I thought the askaris deserved a party, or *ngoma*. The brigade had no further use for us and we had a few days before we could return to Kenya, so I arranged to buy a steer and a supply of millet, to be fermented for *pombe*. Then tragedy struck.

The British NCOs had also done well, as I found they always did when there was plenty going on. When there wasn't enough to do, they were a great trial, especially as I was far from being a martinet. This was just such an occasion. One sergeant had gone to collect the rations and returned very late to say there had been an accident and two askaris had been killed. His story of the accident just didn't wash and I told him it would be much better in the long run to have the truth. It turned out that he had been chasing a buck well off the road and had managed to turn the truck over, killing two of the men in the back. I eventually got a statement which contained nothing but the truth, even if this was a little economical.

I did not relish visiting the mortuary to identify the bodies. It was the first time I had seen the dead body of someone I knew and the young doctor didn't help by making me witness each broken limb and injury, which he described in lurid detail. I only just managed to last it out and reach the fresh air under my own power. The bodies were then cleared for burial and I was advised that, owing to the heat, they should be buried as soon as possible after sunrise next morning. A place in the Christian graveyard was allocated and I found that I was also responsible for digging the graves. A digging party was laid on but it was hard, stony ground and progress painfully slow. By sunset, the graves were only about three feet deep.

By this stage I thought that I really understood the askaris and was amazed when they adamantly refused to continue digging after sunset. Argument was useless—this was some tribal taboo far stronger than army discipline. Since a priest was to meet us at sunrise next morning, there was no alternative but for me and the British NCOs to finish the task. I attacked the ground with great energy and suddenly seemed to have broken through the stony layer as my pick sank in deeply. The next strike met something a little more solid. As I levered it up, I saw it was a human skull. Eventually, in almost total darkness, we finished the gruesome job.

Of course, nothing could alter the tragedy of two young men dying in the prime of life but, nevertheless, it was a strangely moving and beautiful scene as our little group gathered in the small stone-walled cemetery, the vast dusty plain still relatively cool as the sun rose over the foothills of the great Abyssinian massif, with the sounds of the little town going about its normal morning's work. I felt it fitting that these sons of Africa should be returned to their native soil to become part of the great cycle of birth, death and rebirth they understood so well.

The only priest available was Roman Catholic. I had presumed that he would read the burial service for both men, though one was not a Roman Catholic, and was taken aback when he refused. So, as a serving officer, it was my duty to read the service for the Methodist. There being no Kiswahili prayer book available, I had to translate direct from my officer's pocket-book. I did my best to make it as reverent and relevant as possible but would have been happier had I not asked our only English-speaking askari if it was OK. He replied, 'Yes, Bwana, but you actually said "Manure to manure and stones to stones."'

After this, it was obvious that the *ngoma* should be called off in deference to the two dead men. But the African logic was not the same as mine. A deputation of African NCOs came to ask me why I had cancelled it and looked at me with incomprehension when I tried to explain. At last my African sergeant, who best understood the extraordinary workings of the white man's mind, was able to tell me that for them this was an extra special reason for a *ngoma*, as a happy send-off for the spirits of the dead askaris. The party was on again and millet continued to ferment in the forty-gallon oil drum.

Putting on the *ngoma* in the first place had been very much an act of faith that I could rely on my men to behave reasonably, even under the influence of a bellyful of native beer. Now, my confidence eroded by the loss of the rifles, the deaths and the askaris' unexpected refusal to dig the graves, I began to worry.

The first trial was purely physical and I did at least know what to expect—but I also knew that, if I had a phobia, it concerned sharp knives and blood. At the opening ceremony I, *in loco* chief, sat on the edge of the arena while the Africans lined up, each with his machete in his hand. Then, as the drums began to beat, each in turn charged to make a mock attack on the 'chief', cutting the air with great whirling sweeps of their razor-sharp pangas within inches of my nose. In order not to lose their respect, and the prestige of the whole unit, I knew I must not move a muscle, even when I could feel the wind as each panga flashed past. Mick was magnificent, lying nonchalantly under my chair, assuring me that none of the askaris had a grudge against me and all had complete control of their pangas. At last it was over and I was able to make a dignified withdrawal and watch from the sidelines.

Obviously, the lack of women rather cramped the party's style. Even so, there was a lot of drumming and wild dancing and singing, making a disco (not yet invented) seem a very tame affair. Eventually, the last of the steer was eaten and all the *pombe* drunk, with no untoward incidents, and all was a blessed silence. It was a relief when, next morning, everyone was on parade looking reasonably civilised.

There had, of course, to be courts of enquiry into the loss of the rifles and the death of the askaris. I found this rather horrifying: the loss of the rifles was considered so serious that I was told I was extremely lucky not to have to face a court martial, while the death of the askaris, which I considered might well deserve a trial for manslaughter, was deemed quite unimportant.

Just as we were leaving, I developed toothache, only to find that the nearest dentist was at Berbera, about a hundred miles off our route. We weren't in a particular hurry, so when we were level with Berbera we selected a good campsite and I set off with two British NCOs who wanted to come. It didn't take long in an unladen truck and I hoped to get back that night. Alas, the dentist was on safari and we had to wait two more days. The NCOs were put up in the sergeants' mess but I felt responsible for them and set off to find some suitable entertainment, soon discovering that I could hire a dhow for some deep-sea fishing. I returned full of enthusiasm, only to find they weren't the least interested and just wanted to swim in the sergeants' mess pool. This was about the size of four domestic baths and didn't look much fun to me. I then found a safe sea bathing beach inside the coral reef and suggested this, but no, it was still the mess pool. I had a glorious sea bathe by myself.

Once more back on the road, this time with a gap in my front teeth that lasted for the rest of the war. Soon we were back in the comfortable transit camp in Mogadishu and, as customary, I made sure that the askaris were fixed up before finding my allotted hut. On opening it, I was met by a breathtakingly beautiful African girl, tall and graceful, with a lovely figure and a head of black, curly hair. (The Kikuyu women at this time had shaven heads.) I needn't say what my thoughts were: though well brought up and very innocent, I didn't lack hormones. In came Dahir.

'This is my sister whom you promised you would take back to Kenya.'

Now Dahir was an ugly, though attractive, young man but nevertheless there was a remarkable family likeness between them—she even had the same impish grin—and I accepted his story. To do what I did the next day shows how impossibly naive I must have been. I took this lovely girl with me to the HQ of the British Military Administration, explaining that she was my orderly's sister and I wanted her to come back to Kenya in my convoy. Each officer in turn made it quite clear, with an 'oh yeah?' expression, that he did not believe my story and passed me on to the next officer. I was getting more and more frustrated and was about to give up when I was sent to the only black commissioned officer in the East African forces. He didn't give me the raised eyebrow or the 'oh yeah?' expression but merely said that the documentation would take a little time and would not be ready by the time my convoy left, but they would make arrangements to return her to her village in due course. His name must have been Solomon. I hope he had a successful career in the KAR.

We expected to be back in Nanyuki well before Christmas, though the accident truck had been a write-off and two others had to be towed until we could get spare parts. All went reasonably well until we had re-crossed the Juba river. Now, back in the volcanic ash plain, there had been an extraordinary change. It had rained heavily, the dry lifeless plain had vanished and instead we were in a green Garden of Eden. The 'dead' bushes were in leaf, the ground was covered with young grass and flowers and, incredibly, the whole area was alive with zebra, giraffe and antelope, all completely unworried by our convoy. I stopped just to look at this miracle. Some of the animals moved a little further off but the zebra stayed grazing away within a few yards of the road. Then a shot rang out, pandemonium ensued and within seconds the plain was empty except for one zebra which keeled over, thrashed furiously for a few seconds and then lay still. I rushed back to the last truck, driven by the British MT corporal.

'What the hell did you do that for? You know they won't eat zebra meat.'

'For sport, sir.'

Once again I wondered why God had not destroyed the entire human race in the flood.

That night Dahir insisted on putting up my mosquito net, which I considered quite unnecessary. Next morning I had to agree with him. I spent a peaceful night while the NCOs, who wouldn't take good advice, looked as though they had had an attack of super measles.

We soon discovered another major problem. In places the roads had been completely washed away by the rains, turning into, at best, a bog, and at worst a rushing stream. As leading truck, I had to assess each gap, sometimes optimistically crashing through, sometimes getting out for a quick reconnaissance, and quite frequently organising a party of askaris to rebuild the road. More than once we had to tow out trucks that were stuck. The MT corporal made a useful discovery that in these old trucks you could jam the differential with a spanner, thus making a semi four-wheel drive. All this took a lot of time. One day we only managed twenty miles and our already sickly vehicles were put under tremendous strain. When we at last reached drier ground, my truck sounded more like a huge marine diesel and I feared for its life every time we started up. Then there was a great bang. For a few yards it went blissfully smoothly before belching clouds of smoke and steam. In the road behind was a trail of oil leading back to a large piece of metal and one complete piston. We still had eleven trucks but now five of them had to be towed.

As we approached Nanyuki, I began to feel that it would be quite nice to be back in my field company and to have someone to turn to, so the buck didn't always stop with me. I was twenty-one and responsibility was weighing heavily on me. With some relief, we reached our familiar little camp by the river—almost like coming home again—only to find that it was locked and deserted and we were homeless. Military HQ informed me that our field company had been disbanded. We no longer existed and no one had bothered to tell us. It appeared that intercommunication had not improved since the Crimea. Eventually we received orders: my section was to be broken up, those due for leave were to take it and everyone was posted somewhere, but no longer as a unit. The only report that had got back from Abyssinia was that I had lost two rifles and so I was hauled up before further courts of enquiry. The fact that we had done a first-class job demonstrating and teaching about mines was not noticed. I was given fourteen days embarkation leave, which I assumed meant that I would at last be joining the EA Division in Burma.

I rang up Russ Wollen, Ann's father, who was now coffee controller in Nairobi. He very kindly asked me to spend my leave with the family on their farm at Limuru, about fifteen miles out of Nairobi. He also solved my transport problem by leaving Ann and his ancient little Austin Seven at the Muthaiga Club in Nairobi for me to pick up. Once again, showing off let me down. For months I had been driving nothing but heavy trucks (there was no powered steering in those days) and of course the little Austin handled rather differently. Ann beside me, I started outside the club with great verve and, at the end of the drive, swung the wheel as if still in my Chev, resulting in a complete U-turn and back to the club.

The fortnight at the Wollens' farm was an oasis in my life: fourteen days in a real home, with Russ and Maisie making me feel completely at ease, almost as if I was a member of the family. Updown was a typical little settler bungalow, built of wood and thatch, with a reasonably large living room and master bedroom, a kitchen and bathroom. As each child started to grow up, a little thatched hut was built for them near, but not attached to, the original building. As they had four children, so there were four huts and I had one of the boys' while they were away at school. The days were just not long enough, starting with glorious rides through the gentle Limuru hills and valleys, then lovely meals, often on the lawn under the cool shade of the pepper tree, and sometimes a bathe in the small dam just below the house. (This provided sufficient flow and drop to run a turbine for electric light.)

I was also put to work. The farm was on a series of hills and valleys and any ploughed land was subject to serious erosion during the rains. It was therefore contour-ploughed by *bibi* (young women) using power mattocks. Contour-ploughing was not a native tradition and didn't come easily to them, so the terraces had to be lined up and levelled off by a foreman, using the old system of parallel levelling boards. I found this unnecessarily slow: although *bibis* were in plentiful supply, there was always a bottleneck at the working face. By constructing a series of stepped levelling boards, however, I could work on three levels simultaneously. I am not sure if this was actually quicker in the end as for some reason the *bibis* thought it, or I, so hilariously funny that they wasted much energy in convulsive giggles.

I could always borrow the Austin Seven to take Ann into Nairobi for a dinner dance at the Muthaiga Club or to the cinema. The little, very ancient Austin had long since lost its self-starter but always started on the first turn of the handle. One dark, moonless night we came out of the cinema. The antique engine answered obediently first time but, as soon as the lights were switched on, cut out. Here was a problem. It was not proper to take my host's sixteen year-old daughter to a hotel for the night but, on the other hand, to return to Limuru we had to drive fifteen miles up the escarpment road, with a precipitous drop on one side, only protected by the occasional large stone.

We set out optimistically and all was well in the town until the streetlights ended. Now it was just not possible to go on. I left the car and followed a light that led me to an African hut. As I was now fairly fluent in Swahili, I managed to persuade the owner to lend me a hurricane lamp. The next problem was how to fix the lamp to the car. This was soon solved with my shoelace and we proceeded—only to run into another problem. At speeds greater than seven miles per hour, the lamp blew out, so we had to drive at six and a half. We arrived back eventually to find a very worried mother and father.

Updown was a small farm. It supplemented Russ's job as coffee controller, growing enough maize to feed the stock, which included their horses, two or three cows, a few goats, a sty of pigs and some chickens. There were two Italian prisoners-of-war working on the farm, nice men who were only too glad to get away from the war and the crowded prison-camps. One of their specialities was a gorgonzola-like cheese that the Wollens thought was great but was not quite to my taste. Before the Italians were repatriated, they gave the Wollens the recipe, after which their taste for the cheese diminished.

Recipe for Italian POW Cheese: Allow milk to sour, drain off whey, wrap curds in cloth. Collect buckets of droppings from stables, cowshed, goat shed, pig sty and chicken run. Pack barrel with alternate layers of mixed droppings and curds, allow to mature, eat quickly before it takes off.

The pony that I had looked at in Nanyuki had settled down quite well, though he was still a bit nervous. We had one difference of opinion over crossing a narrow, five-foot deep irrigation channel. He reared up on his hind legs, at the same time swivelling round. The bank collapsed, his hind legs slipped into the ditch and I slowly slid down his back, ending up wedged in an upside-down, touching-toes position, and causing a most effective dam in the channel.

All too soon my leave was over and I reported to a transit camp about one and a half miles from Nairobi. There was little constructive to do—I had already left my dear Mick with Mu and the roguish Dahir was still on leave—but this was offset by the exciting expectation of soon joining the EA Division in Burma and perhaps meeting up with old comrades. In the evenings, meanwhile, we could get out to the cinema or a hotel, usually ending with a rickshaw race back to the camp, which was all downhill.

The idea of rickshaw races came from a bored young officer (guess who). After hiring your rickshaw, you persuaded the driver to sit in the cab and each competing officer got between the shafts. By moving forwards or back, you could balance the cart so that you were almost weightless; thus trimmed and going downhill you could get up a great speed, taking enormously long strides.

Chapter Eight

After a few weeks, we took the train to Mombasa and boarded the Polaski, an extremely ancient and battered coal-burning ship that had managed to escape from Poland when she was invaded. The troop decks were bad enough, though with some ventilation, but the officers' cabins, with six in a two-berth cabin, no ventilation and portholes that didn't open, were impossible to live in while we were sailing along the equator. However, we were allowed to sleep out on the boat deck. We shared this honour with the girls, made up of Wrens, Ats and nurses, but in the interests of propriety we were separated by wire netting and a door that was locked at night. Sometimes the tropical nights were unbelievably bright with stars, so that you could almost read. Except for a phosphorescent glow where the bows ploughed through the warm sea there were no lights showing, though sometimes you could just make out the dim shape of our destroyer escort. One hot sticky overcast night sleep was impossible. I walked round the deck and noticed a ventilation port with a little door in it. It was unlocked, opening on to a dimly-lit shaft, down which ran an iron ladder.

Obviously this called for further investigation. I pulled a pair of trousers over my sarong and went down. As I suspected, it led to the engine room. Quite a current of air was coming down the shaft and, despite the coal furnaces and huge boilers, it felt cooler than on deck. The Polish crew didn't mind my presence and were prepared to talk but in the absence of a common language we didn't get very far. In due course I made the long climb back up the shaft and found my pile of clothes and bedding. As I pushed back the blanket, there was a high-pitched scream. Within seconds I was back in the shaft, now realising that there was a shaft on either side of the wire netting. I didn't dare make enquiries next day but I often wonder if someone woke from a nightmare or from what they thought was an exciting dream.

In the daytime our bedroom, with the gate unlocked, became a parade ground for a twice-daily boat drill. In between these drills it was used as a sports deck shared by the women, officers and white NCOs. I suppose I must have been sports officer—at any rate, it fell to me to organise some friendly sparring for any who wished. One who wished was a large and tough girl, Pam, whose father ran one of the Bovril ranches in Argentina. She had a pretty lethal punch but all the men were too chivalrous to hit back, making it a bit one-sided.

One of the NCOs had, I think, been bet that he couldn't knock out one of the officers. Being the only officer taking part, I agreed to have a 'friendly' bout with him. It was soon clear that it was not friendly and he landed an extremely hard punch. Convinced that I was the better boxer, I decided to play it his way and was just beginning to get some good punches in when he broke it off, complaining of a sore hand. I was not altogether sorry to learn next day that he had actually broken a finger on my head. (I suspect that some padding had been removed from the glove.)

One of the Africans died on voyage of a medical condition and, naturally, was buried at sea. As befitted a soldier in the Imperial Army, his shroud was draped in a Union Jack and, as he was a Christian, a dignified committal was read in English. Then the platform on which he lay was tipped and the shrouded body slid from under the flag and, even though the Captain had temporarily reduced speed, soon plunged into the rapidly retreating foam. For a maritime race, burial at sea seems natural, as it were to join in spirit Kipling's 'Jolly, Jolly Mariners'. But somehow, for a son of Africa, he was pathetically alone and it seemed wrong that he should not return to his native soil.

After three weeks at sea, we steamed slowly into Colombo harbour with a great feeling of excitement, not only because of the beauty of Ceylon but also because surely, at last, we were getting to the war. The Free French battleship Richelieu was also steaming in. To add to the anticipation, the harbour was packed with shipping, including naval vessels and landing-craft. Obviously a great offensive was in preparation, in which we hoped we would be taking part. (In fact, shortly afterwards, most of the landing-craft were withdrawn to be used in the Normandy landings.)

Suddenly two Hurricanes appeared, making a mock dive-bombing attack on the Richelieu, but something went tragically wrong. At the climax of their power dives, when the bombs would have been released, their wing tips just touched and within a split second both planes had disintegrated. For a few more seconds small fragments crashed into the harbour, then all was silence. Gradually the full horror and waste of war ate into one's soul.

Colombo was a beautiful city and seemed, after three weeks in a troopship, incredibly full of colour, life and interest. Though hot, there was a slight sea breeze but we hadn't long to admire it as the EAE contingent was sent off to a coconut plantation near Kurunagala. *Good points:* beautiful flowers amongst the grass, an ample supply of coconuts, lots of geckos and lizards, a good loo (see later) and, at first, the expectation that this was only a staging-post for Burma. *Bad points:* though almost at sea level, it was well inland and hot, humid and airless (though temperatures seldom went above thirty-two degrees C, it was so humid that at night, clad only in a sarong, one was running sweat); we had no tent or building, only a tarpaulin; the view in every direction was coconut palms; we were not a unit but just Reinforcements of all ranks; finally, with virtually no equipment, it was impossible to get down to any real training.

Gradually, as the novelty of being in a new environment began to wear off and the hope of immediate posting seemed more and more remote, we stagnated into sweaty frustration. Everything was so uncertain. If we had known that we were to be here for six months, we could have been constructive and even studied local fauna and flora, but every week a trickle of officers was posted and we each hoped that we would be next. This turned out to be the most depressing period of my army career. I felt more and more useless and unwanted. Surely I hadn't trained for over four years just to die of boredom under a tarpaulin in a humid coconut plantation? One East Africa-born officer spent most of the day on his bed drinking gin and water and periodically yelling for his orderly to come a hundred yards from his quarters to fill his glass. (I must add that there were some first class EA-born officers!)

I was saved from quite such depravity and mental decay by an interest in the local fauna. A colony of kabaragoyers, huge aquatic lizards up to seven feet long, were based in a local irrigation tank and often came through the camp. They were said to be quite harmless but if we met one when swimming in the tank we got out remarkably quickly. In retrospect, I think we were at much more risk from sundry tropical parasites and diseases in the tank water.

Then there was the loo. This was situated half-way up an isolated mound, almost at coconut palm-top level, giving a change of view (the tops of coconut palms rather than the trunks) in every direction and just a suspicion of cooler, though not always fresher, air. It had a box seat covering the hole, a low matting screen and a fly swat. The latter was much used and every time a hit was scored and a fly fell to the ground, the resident lizard shot out to clear it away. (A more constructive/destructive occupation than reading the paper, especially as we only got the weekly edition of *The News of the World*.)

There was also a large colony of fruit bats as large as small owls which would attack any fruit left uncovered under our mess tarpaulin. They were a bit creepy until you got used to them. Lastly, there were crows, which would often come into the mess looking for food. One evening, by way of experiment, we put some bits of bread soaked in local brandy just outside the mess. The crows arrived but one boss crow chased all the others off, consuming almost all the bread himself. With the bread finished, they flew off but the overloaded boss crow had difficulty in taking off and turned a complete somersault. He then picked himself up, flew on to a low shrub and perched there, rocking backwards and forwards until he eventually fell off and flapped into the undergrowth.

Otherwise, the monotony was only broken by an occasional visit to a curry restaurant. Ceylonese curries were hotter than their Indian counterpart, with the additional danger that a sip of the accompanying palm spirit, arrack, instead of cooling you down was even more fiery.

I did manage to get to a bridging course at Roorkee, about 1,500 miles away in northern India. I travelled up with Ian, also in the EAE and an occasional bridge partner in transit camps or at sea. After a couple of days of very comfortable first class travel on Indian Railways we arrived at Roorkee, only to find that someone had blundered and the course wasn't due to start for another week. It seemed ridiculous to return to Ceylon so, as senior officer of all two of us,

I posted us on a week's leave and authorised a coach voucher to the hill station of Mussouree, a hundred-odd miles away in the foothills of the Himalayas.

Roorkee was in the very hot, dusty plain, with midday temperatures at this time of year up to forty-six degrees C, and the overcrowded bus was almost unbearable. At last we began to see the hills in the distance and suddenly we were climbing steeply, with the oppressive weight of heat lifting from us as the air became clearer and less dusty. At the end of the motorable road, where we stopped just below the bright clean hill town, the bus was surrounded by dozens of small tough hill men, competing to be our porters. (We were the only passengers with much luggage. Mine consisted of a valise containing a wooden-framed camp-bed and bedding, plus folding camp basin, a suitcase and a small ammunition case of books. Ian's was similar. When we changed trains at Madras we had two porters, who complained it was too heavy for them.) There was a sort of free fight amongst the porters until one man seemed to emerge victorious from the mêlée. We presumed he would act as portage foreman but not at all. The others dispersed and he laid a strap on the ground, placed all our luggage on it, lay on his back, looped the strap over his head and got to his feet, carrying the lot. He asked which hotel we were going to, pointed to it (about a hundred yards up a one-in-three slope) and took off at a steady trot, leaving us panting after him. On arrival, we were both going to tip him but he was quite content with what I gave him and went off.

After the dripping heat of Kurunagala and the oven-like heat of the Indian plain, Mussouree was heaven. Mostly we did little but enjoy feeling cool, with an occasional ride around in a tonga. One day we heard there was to be tonga-pony racing, so we walked to the meeting which was held on the only flat ground near the town. The races were all short and without jumps, and mostly confined to the ponies' owners, but one race was billed as open. I decided to have a go. I found a likely-looking pony and asked if I could borrow him for the race. I was, of course, rather heavy for the little animal. A white jockey caused quite a sensation and I was heavily backed. I don't know whether to blame my weight, my choice of pony, lack of understanding of local language or just bad horsemanship but it turned out to be a very good race for the bookies.

The first two miles of the journey back to Roorkee were a little hairy, the essentially single-track road descending 4,000 feet in a series of hairpins, with super views and precipitous drops. Sensibly, it was one-way traffic on alternate hours. I know not who was at fault but we met two cars coming up. To this day it remains a mystery how we got past.

Roorkee was oppressively hot but we had four hours off in the hottest part of the day. This was OK for the staff in their huts but not for the pupils in tents, which were lethal at this time of day. Our mess hut was only a little better. If there was even a suspicion of wind, one could sit under a tree but, if not, the only solution was to move slowly around, creating your own air movement. Though I learned little new on the course, it was good exercise and I hoped it might help with a posting.

The bridging was hard physical work, each man carrying up to one hundred pounds. The larger girders were carried by teams of six, taking the weight on hollow steel pipes held across their arms, but working in any clothing above the waist was impossible in this heat and the iron pipes were untouchable. The solution was to work in parties of seven, with the spare man carrying a bucket and six wet sacks. Yes, it was hot but surprisingly reasonable if you had plenty of water. We stopped for a drink three times each hour, when it was not unusual to put down two pints of slightly salted water. Apart from a few burns from the hot steel, we were quite fit, though in the three weeks I lost ten kilograms.

The bridging was on the irrigation canal, along which ran a pilgrim route. They came in a constant stream, some walking, some crawling and some on their knees, often with horrible sores; occasionally one walked in short stages on his hands only. I never discovered where they went and what merit they acquired but it did not appeal to me as a path to salvation.

Chapter Nine

Returning to Ceylon, we caught an early train, changing at a remote junction where we were told that our connection wasn't running and the next train was in eight hours. There was a reasonably cool waiting-room, shared only by two Indians. More in hope than expectation, and with a shameful degree of arrogance, we asked if they played bridge.

'Oh yes.'

'Contract bridge?'

'Oh yes.'

We started the game without having agreed for what stakes we were playing—usually four annas per thousand. (There are sixteen annas in a rupee, which was then worth about one shilling and sixpence, at least £1 in modern value.) They suggested ten rupees. Not to seem too mean, we got it down to one rupee, four times our usual. It turned out that they were a minor maharajah and his agent. By the time our connection arrived, we were seventy-five rupees up and wishing we had accepted their original stake.

Then it was back to Ceylon again and the frustration of being a Reinforcement, even hoping at times to step into a dead man's shoes.

One afternoon, four of us managed to get a lift to Kandy, a lovely town much higher and cooler than Kurunagala, where Admiral (Lord) Mountbatten, Commander in Chief, South East Asia Command, had his headquarters. It was always said that to be on his staff a man had to be brilliant and a girl had to be both brilliant and very pretty. We found that there was a dance at the Empress Hotel and naturally went to see.

We were not disappointed. The ballroom was full of lovely girls from all the services but, alas, they showed not the least interest in junior Reinforcement officers, having been well dated up by innumerable senior staff officers. All we could do was to drown our frustration at the bar and feast our eyes on things rather more shapely than coconut palms.

In one of the passages leading to the dance floor someone spotted a waiter's bicycle. One of our group bet anyone a bottle of brandy to ride the bicycle once round the floor. I was merry enough to take up the challenge (a court martial seemed vastly preferable to rotting away in Reinforcements) and I was quite sober enough to weave skilfully in and out of the dancing couples and return to claim my reward. At this moment the DAPM (shorthand for the Military Police Captain) appeared. He recognised us for what we were, a lot of frustrated and bored young men, and having accepted a drink from my bottle gave me a brotherly talk and advised me not to appear in Kandy again in the near future. We took ourselves off to a Chinese restaurant and then returned to Kurunagala.

Next morning I wasn't feeling too good—but then I had been rather over-indulging. The second day I felt worse, and on the third day even worse, and was by now passing a lovely mature port-coloured urine. A visit to the medical officer produced a diagnosis of infective jaundice and I was despatched to the hospital in Kandy.

For a couple of days I just lay in bed, doing and wanting nothing. On the third day I felt strong enough to look round. I was in a cool clean ward of about twelve beds on the ground floor, looking out on another coconut plantation—but this time with a great difference. A team of elephants with their mahouts were pulling up and removing the trees. Chains were fixed to the coconut palms, about six feet from the ground, then one or more of the elephants pulled. With a little help from a coolie with a mattock, the trees were uprooted and dragged away.

After a time, I looked round the ward. There were eleven other men in various stages of illness. The face in the next bed seemed rather familiar. Where had I met him? The scene changed: the striped pyjamas became a captain's uniform, the ward a dance floor, the jug of water a bottle of brandy... After the first shock of meeting, we became the best of friends. Before joining the military police, he had been ten years in the London Metropolitan Police, mostly with the Vice Squad, and was an interesting and entertaining companion.

Military hospitals have to be experienced to be believed. As always, one was woken very early and washed and fed. Then, at 0900 hours precisely (for our ward) the hospital sergeant-major called the ward to 'Atten-SHUN!' Those caught standing stood stiffly at attention, those sitting sat bolt upright and those in bed lay stiff as ramrods until we were stood easy while the Chief Medical Officer carried out his round.

I don't suppose that blood tests had been invented, so we were spared those and I don't remember any treatment except diet. This never varied: a cup of tea without milk twice daily, while for the three main meals you were given a jug of boiling water, several slices of dry bread and a pot of marmite. In addition, half a grapefruit at breakfast and a half pint of Guinness at supper. However, the lack of humanity was made up for by a lovely coloured nurse who smiled sweetly at all without fear or favour and with whom we were, to a man, much in love.

Because of, or despite, the diet, I began to improve and after three weeks was sent to a convalescent camp in the hills. I only hoped that I wouldn't miss a posting to Burma, though I had to admit that I felt about as strong as a bruised dandelion stalk. The journey to Diatalawa was by train and I found myself (per-haps, more truthfully, *put* myself) in a compartment with three ATS officers. I was still sore at being stuck in Reinforcements and obviously thought it was the sole fault of the Divisional Commander that so suit-able an officer had not been sent for. At any rate, we got talking about the progress of the war and EA Division and, with all the authority of a junior sub-altern, I voiced no confidence in the Divisional Com-mander. One of the girls seemed interested and asked who I thought should replace him. Without hesita-tion, I suggested Brigadier Dimoline who, despite referring to me as 'that bloody sapper umpire', had greatly impressed me on a Kilimanjaro exercise. The young lady seemed extremely interested, as well as being rather attractive, so before she got out at the next station I asked her name.

'Betty Dimoline.'

It was a pleasant three weeks at Diatalawa and some of my strength returned, though it took two or three years to feel really fit again. Mostly I read and relaxed but two days before I left I found a pre-war tourist guide. It described a remote guest house from which you 'looked down on another world 5,000 feet below' and where supper and bed and breakfast were quite cheap. You could only get there by train but there was a service both ways morning and evening. I managed to enthuse two other officers and one of them produced three girls from the women's convalescent camp. We collected a packed lunch and caught the early train.

When we reached our destination, we found the station was in a deep canyon with a long tunnel at either end. As far as we could see, the only way out was a steep and narrow path leading up the side of the cliff. For some time the path led up through thickish jungle, eventually levelling out on to a great plain covered with shrub and scrub. A rough, often overgrown path led, we hoped, the eight or nine miles to the guest house. At last we arrived, tired and hungry, to find it boarded up and deserted. The view was stupendous and well worth the walk but, obviously, we had to get back for the evening train.

After eating our packed lunch, we set off at a moderate pace until one of the girls badly twisted her ankle, greatly reducing our speed. It soon became clear that, at this pace, we would not reach the station in time. She was a fairly petite young lady and I was the largest of the men, so the only solution was for me to take her pick-a-back. The rough ground and my still rather weak state definitely delayed us and the other two men didn't seem able to carry her. At last we reached the top of the cliff path, just in time to see the train pulling out of the station. By the time we reached the empty platform, the station master had locked up and would not let us remain in the (anyhow quite inadequate) ticket office. There was no train until early next morning and it was beginning to get dark and very cold. The station master said our only hope was to return up the cliff path to where an Englishman and his wife were living. So, once more back up the path, very slowly this time. We had not noticed the house before but by now it was dark and we could follow the light.

The Reydens were a lovely old couple who had retired up here after his lifetime as a Columbo harbour pilot. They scratched up a very adequate meal for us, but bedding was somewhat limited. The three girls shared a two-bed bedroom; the men's dormitory had no beds, only the house supply of carpets in the form of animal skins. My ration was one antelope's and one leopard's skin and the night was neither warm nor comfortable but infinitely preferable to freezing on the platform.

We were woken with a cup of tea while it was still dark. Our host and hostess insisted that the jungle was full of leopards and therefore they must accompany us to the station. Mrs Reyden led the way, armed with a 45 revolver, and he took up the rear with a big game rifle.

Two mornings later, I was on the early train, returning to Kurunagala. As we had consumed so much of the Reydens' reserves, I had promised to get any replacements I could through the NAAFI shop and drop them off at the station. I managed to acquire quite a large wooden crate of suitable tins. As the train emerged from the tunnel, there was Mrs Reyden on the platform, mounted on a large horse, her revolver sticking out of her belt. The horse, in protest at the train's whistle, reared up on its hind legs, while the train, full of servicemen and women, burst into singing 'Pistol-packing Momma'. To this accompaniment, I solemnly marched up the platform to hand over my box. How she negotiated the cliff path, I just don't know.

Back at Kurunagala, things were beginning to

happen. Several other officers had gone sick and the Africans were rather unkindly saying that we must be going to war as all the white men were going to hospital. We moved to another camp with palm thatched huts—more comfortable but without the interest of the kabaragoyers. We were still not a proper unit and I knew very few of the Africans but there was one event that was to help me later: one of the askaris went berserk.

This was not that unusual. Coming straight from a fairly simple tribal existence, the askaris had to undergo a tremendous amount of adaptation to modern army life, especially in a technical unit. On this particular occasion, one had occupied a high mound in the centre of the camp and was threatening to shoot anyone who came near him. (We had been training with live ammunition and each askari had an issue of ten rounds.) I was glad that he was not my responsibility as I had no idea how to deal with the situation. I just wondered what I would have done if I were in charge and for the moment kept out of sight. Various people tried to reason with him but to no avail, except to have his rifle pointed at them, coupled with the unmistakable sound of a live

303 cartridge going into the breech of a Lee-Enfield, and a hasty retreat. Then the African sergeant-major came out, completely ignored the sound of loading but kept up a conversation something like this:

'We are all going to the war soon and we may well get killed. So kill me now if you like, but it would be much better first to kill a few Japs who have killed our brothers.'

All the time, he continued to walk calmly towards the hillock. When he was quite close, the askari dropped his rifle and went off with him.

Soon after this, we really were on the move. First, a few days of jungle-training in the wildest area of northern Ceylon. We arrived just as it was getting dark in the camp, which was surrounded by jungle. By the time I had seen that the askaris had suitable accommodation and a meal preparing, I came to the officers' quarters to find that all the huts had been bagged. The orderly said he would take me to the reserve huts. He led the way for about a hundred yards down a path so overgrown that he had to clear most of it with a panga while I held a hurricane lamp. Eventually we arrived at a timber-and-thatch block of cubicles, separated by palm matting. No doors but probably waterproof. We selected the cleanest and put up my camp bed and mosquito net.

After supper at the mess, I returned down the jungle path with my lamp. It felt, I must admit, a little creepy and rather isolated from civilisation but I was soon comfortably asleep under my net, with the extra security of my loaded revolver under my pillow, its lanyard round my wrist. I was a light sleeper and suddenly was wide awake—to the sound of deep breathing. For a moment I thought that someone was standing by my bed but soon realised that the breathing was from the next cubicle. How could anyone have arrived without waking me?

I had to investigate but had first to light my lamp. Then, lamp in one hand and my revolver in the other, I advanced slowly until I could see round into the next cubicle. There, standing peacefully facing the doorway, was a huge water buffalo, looking at me without a sign of aggression in his limpid brown eyes. I was soon happily asleep again and for the next few nights slept very lightly until my companion came in.

I was asked to revise map-reading and compass marching with the British NCOs, of whom there were about twenty. Most were as demoralised as I was with life as a Reinforcement and showed very little interest in the subject. This brought out my worst bloody-mindedness. I sent them out about six miles by truck and set them off in pairs to find their way back to the camp through a particularly difficult bit of jungle, where the tracks led in almost any but the right direction. I also set out, with one NCO, and arrived safely at the camp, thanks much more to having a very good sense of direction than to careful compass plotting. We were back hours before anyone else and I grew more and more worried when no one arrived. Eventually some of them did turn up, while others managed to get back to the start, from where we collected them. Next day my class paid much more attention.

Then we were on the move again, crossing the Palk Strait to India. Our small ferry gave us a super view of the shallow water teeming with fish, particularly huge rays with six-foot wing spans. At last we arrived at a transit camp in Calcutta. This was something like a departure lounge in that you had finally been processed and were just waiting to board a ship. It would have been nice to have been going with a unit and men that you knew but at least, I thought, it was a welcome relief to have no responsibility. Early in the morning we boarded a small coastal cargo-cum-passenger steamer on the Hooghli river.

Chapter Ten

The anatomy of the little steamer on the Hooghli is important to the next incident, so I will describe it in some detail. There were two decks of cabins, with the bridge above. Forward of the bridge, the decks were cut away to give access to the cargo hatch and forward again was a forecastle, above which was mounted a loaded anti-aircraft machine gun. The top deck was for officers, the second for British NCOs and the hold for African NCOs and men.

I was watching the river with all its variety of little craft when I noticed everyone crowding forward to peer into the hold area. Looking down, I saw that an askari had gone berserk and had drawn his razor-sharp panga in his right hand and held a sinister knife in the left. As soon as anyone tried to enter the area, he rushed at them with great sweeps of the panga, giving the distinct impression he meant to use it. My phobia of sharp knives made my flesh creep. But, after all, this was no concern of mine. I just wondered idly what action I would advise if asked and decided that, given time, he would probably settle down. At this moment, a ship's officer tapped me on the shoulder.

'As the [only] officer in the East African contingent, will you please get him out of the way? The crew refuse to go forward to raise the anchor and we must sail with the tide.'

Reality came as a great shock. For a moment I could hardly breathe but there was no time to waste: I must face that flashing panga. Adrenalin began to take over and my mind cleared as I ran down the companion ways to the hatch deck. As I came out of the doorway, the askari charged at me, panga raised menacingly. I

have never been more terrified but, remembering the incident at Kurunagala, I knew I must show no fear. I walked slowly towards him, trying to keep my voice calm and my hands at my sides.

'We are all off to the war, so it's better to keep your panga for the Japs.'

For a moment he hesitated, panga still raised above his head, well within striking distance.

'I am your friend. What is the trouble?'

Slowly he lowered the panga and the knife and began to calm down and talk, part in Kiswahili and part in some tribal language, to the effect that *I* was his friend but some other askaris were *shenzi sana* (wild, uncivilised). Before I could get any further, some of the British NCOs on the deck above started to laugh mockingly and all was lost. The askari tore off his jacket, shouting that some people were a disgrace to King George's uniform, and clambered up the ladder to the machine-gun tower, handling the gun as though he knew how to use it. What was more, it covered the deck area and the crew still refused to go forward. Time and tide were not waiting. Clearly, I had lost the first round and other tactics were needed.

I discovered that there was an African corporal of

the same tribe and sent for him in the hope that he might talk the askari down better in his own tribal language. To no avail. Then came an inspiration. The tribal African at this time still thought that much of the white man's magic was contained in the needle, so they were always keen to join an inoculation parade (unlike the British soldier, who would often pass out before even getting to the front of the queue). Luckily, there was a medical orderly on board and with his assistance a queue was formed to the medical cabin. With the help of the African NCO, the askari was talked down with the bribe that he could go to the front of the queue. On arrival, he asked for a drink of water but, when it was produced, insisted that it was poisoned and only drank it after I had had half. Now for the needle. Again, he insisted it might be poisoned, again I offered to have it first, hoping that the medical orderly would understand. He did. As I bared my arm, he selected an enormous needle and, to make sure the askari was watching, sank it slowly and deliberately and painfully up to the hilt in my arm, then went through the motion of injecting it. All was now well. The askari accepted the injection (of morphine) and was soon peacefully asleep.

When I got back on deck, I found I was shaking like a leaf and feeling distinctly sick. The crew now went forward and raised the anchor but it was too late. We were soon stuck fast on a sandbank, where we had to wait for the next tide. As a result, we arrived at Chittagong late the following afternoon.

It seemed, though no one had told me, that I was in charge of the African contingent. We managed to get the askaris, 299 of them, lined up on the quay and called the roll, then divided them into sections, each with an NCO in charge. During the call I received a direct hit from a black kite (not for nothing popularly known as the shite hawk). It was said to be lucky but I reserved judgement.

A party of West Africans had been laid on to guide us to the transit camp, where we were to eat and sleep before boarding a train in the morning. By the time we set out to march there, the light was failing. We crossed a huge marshalling yard (Chittagong was the supply port for much of the 14th Army fighting in Burma) and I was with the last section of twenty-five askaris when we were held up for a good half-hour by a series of trains shunting across the yard. When we eventually arrived at the other side, there was no sign of a single guide or, indeed, a living soul. We were alone, the black-out was deepened by steam from the engines and all was silent except for the occasional train whistle and the clanking of shunting trucks.

At last I found a man operating some points and asked the way to the camp. He pointed rather vaguely in the direction we were going, with no information of how far it was, and we went on, asking anyone we saw. To my great surprise, after about half an hour we arrived at the camp, only to find that the first twenty-five of my charges had arrived with *all* the guides but, except for my own twenty-five, all the other 249 were missing. I was annoyed rather than worried, made sure that there was a meal and somewhere to sleep for the men if and when they arrived and arranged to have them woken in the morning.

It was now 2300 hours and I decided to turn in. At that moment a message arrived to say that we were to march to the station and board a train at 0300 hours. The West African guides were nowhere to be seen and I was still short of 249 men. As I knew none of those who had arrived, I collected three or four NCOs and asked them to pick another batch of intelligent looking askaris. I then sent these out in pairs in all directions, with instructions to search for half an hour only before returning with anyone they could find. At 0200 hours small groups were still arriving. There was no area with enough room and light to make a roll-call possible, and in any case we couldn't do any more to find the absentees, so we set off to the station and packed all we had found into the train. When we arrived at Comilla a day later and were able to call the roll, we were short of one man only and no one seemed the least worried. I often wonder if he ever turned up.

At long last I was posted to 54 Field Company EAE in the 11th East African Division of the 14th (Burma) Army. They had recently been withdrawn from the front for rest and retraining. It was great to have my own platoon again and to start to get to know the NCOs and askaris, but it was not an altogether happy unit. The CO had been retired and the new CO was not popular with the askaris or the other four officers, who anyhow had very little in common. We were camped in close and claustrophobic jungle, with our only tent used for the orderly room. Our mess and sleeping quarters were tarpaulins stretched between the trees and the equipment for training was inadequate. We had enough Bailey bridge parts to throw half a light bridge over a small stream—an operation that my platoon could soon do in the dark, hardly bothering to wake up.

For normal training, the askaris paraded in boots, jungle trousers, cotton singlets and 'safari' hats and if we were working in one place they were allowed to discard their singlets. One day, while we were working on the Bailey bridge with fifty singlets laid out neatly on the ground, a herd of native cattle wandered off the track and before anyone noticed ate four or five of the salt-sweat laden vests. Though now over twenty-one, I was obviously still naïve. I promised that anyone who had lost their vest could draw a new one from the QM store. That evening the QM sergeant issued out fifty new singlets.

On the credit side, we were a very sporting unit and could always raise a football or hockey team from the British officers and NCOs. In soccer, we usually played African teams. They preferred to play barefoot, so to avoid injury we wore gym shoes. Few of our askaris played hockey and we had to find outside opponents. Being engineers and having a bulldozer, we created a pitch out of the jungle. This was really more suitable for soccer than hockey, as the patches where large trees had been removed never quite dried out, sometimes leading to the complete disappearance of the ball, in which case a bully was held on the nearest bit of firm ground. Once, with the help of another field company, we raised a rugger team to contest a match on a dry paddy field, but after a spate of injuries this was banned by the medics.

I also tried my hand at fishing with a hook and line that I had acquired somehow. A small, extremely overgrown stream ran through the camp and by balancing on a fallen tree trunk I could get my line into the water. Despite various baits, there were no takers. I decided to leave the line for a time, coming back later to find it in a complete tangle. Squatting on my tree trunk, I began the long job of disentangling it when suddenly there was a great tug, pulling me off balance. To avoid falling in, I grasped the trunk with both arms. This proved a big mistake as I was bare from the waist up and the tree had bark like sandpaper, resulting in the loss of a great deal of skin from my chest. Having got to my feet, I found that I had caught quite a sizeable fish. I delivered it to the mess cook and proceeded to the medical tarpaulin. The

African dresser was in no doubt as to the treatment and painted my chest with tincture of iodine. (To those who have not met this, it is made up in strong spirit and is extremely painful.)

However, the fish was a welcome change to army rations and we decided to try another method of fishing. A small charge in one of the pools produced several fish. Until now, we had never seen any natives near the camp but clearly they had seen us: next morning a small deputation of Indians arrived. There was no common language but signs showed that it had something to do with a bang and fish. As usual, it was put firmly in my court and since I was obviously expected to follow the leading deputy, I did so. He led me to a big pool and, again with signs, asked me to make another big bang. I sent for a primer and detonator and did what he wanted. Several fish came to the surface and our friend indicated these were mine. Then he and his gang walked into the pool and probed and dived in the muddy water, coming up with about as many fish as we had taken from the surface. From then on we often had fresh fish on the menu, though we always waited until a deputation came to take us to a suitable pool.

Chapter Eleven

As I have said, it was not a happy unit. We officers had little in common, were very different in age and background, even rather disliked each other and were frankly bored. As as a result, we tended to drink too much.

One day a notice appeared on the edge of the track a few hundred yards from our camp, saying 'Site for YMCA Tent'. A few days later a patch of jungle had been cleared. This at least united us in a common cause, as none of us were practising Christians. 'We were f***ing well not going to be preached at by some man too f***ing cowardly to join up! Oh no.'

In due course, a large tent appeared on the site, with red check curtains in the windows. I think it was the curtains that did it. We had all been away from home for several years and were not a little homesick, and a tent with curtains was very much more like home than our tarpaulin. Somehow we just had to go in.

Inside were camp chairs grouped round camp tables, each with a bright cloth. I found myself sitting down with some of my colleagues, whom I disliked, while an old man, far past military service age, brought us cups of tea and persuaded us to play some games (Monopoly, dominoes, draughts, etc). Next evening we again found ourselves there, meeting officers and NCOs from other units, and so it went on for about a fortnight until, one evening, the tent had gone and six weeks later the jungle was rapidly reclaiming the site. Here, surely, was the end of the story. But, incredibly, it wasn't: the whole atmosphere under our tarpaulin was different. We started talking to each other and three of us taught the other two to play bridge. With something to do, we drank less, we got to know one another and I would even say we got to like each other.

This was to have a very profound effect on my life. The old man had not once mentioned 'God' or 'Christ' or 'Religion' and yet he had completely changed our attitude. How? I could only presume that, as he worked for the YMCA, he must be a Christian and this must have something to do with it. I also remembered that at my primary training unit at Ripon there was a YMCA canteen where smiley girls dispensed 'cha and a wad' (tea and a bun) with no strings attached. Why? Perhaps O'Shaughnessy's 'Music Makers' should really have started, 'We are the tea-dispensers/And we are the dreamers of dreams.' My time in Africa with its teeming life and the African's philosophy had already turned me from an atheist to an agnostic; now I was beginning to think that there might be something in Christianity. To start my search, I talked to a Canadian padre, to see if there was any help there. Unfortunately not. His type of Christianity didn't appeal to me. He had a revolver with several notches on it, each representing a Jap he had shot with great pride.

Back in our camp, although the officers were getting on much better, the CO did not have the respect of the askaris. A rather ugly situation developed when an askari refused to carry out an order from the CO and the African NCOs refused to force him to come to the orderly room for the CO summarily to try and sentence him. The other officers did not consider that the CO had been right in the first place but, nevertheless, this was technically mutiny. The situation was handed over to and handled by the Military Police. The whole camp was surrounded by a company of Gurkhas. Our company were made to hand over their rifles, issued with picks and shovels and marched off to another bit of jungle with orders to dig trenches to a certain specification before filling them in again. Meanwhile the CO was tactfully posted elsewhere. We all thought this was a fair solution and rather enjoyed our fortnight of hard labour. In fact, there was keen competition as to which section could dig the fastest trench and some of the officers joined any diggers who were tiring. After a fortnight we returned to our camp a rather fitter and happier unit under a new CO.

Soon after this we packed up and moved to a 'wet bridging' camp on the Ganges near Mongyr. This was a great improvement in almost every way. Firstly, there was adequate equipment for light folding-boat and heavier Bailey pontoon-bridging, and there were two motor boats and enough outboard motors to make raft ferries. Secondly, we were in a tented camp in a shady mango orchard on the bank of the great river, from which we often had a gentle breeze. The Ganges here was in most respects perfect for training, with a hard and wide beach, the steadily flowing river deepening fairly rapidly to about seven or eight feet. It must have been, at the very least, half a mile wide, with a large low shingle bank in the middle.

The snag was that Mongyr, one of the Hindu holy places (and therefore having burning ghats) was a few miles upstream. Hindus were supposed to be cremated and their ashes sprinkled on Mother Ganges. In practice, the corpse had often been brought a long way by very poor people. By the time they reached the river, there was little money left to buy firewood so by necessity, after a mere token fire, the bodies were pushed into the water where they were eventually disposed of by river turtles. Each morning, before work started, a body fatigue was laid on whose job was to launch one of the motor boats and pull any bodies or parts thereof—some almost like dried driftwood, others grotesque and balloon-like—off the beach into mid stream. They were seldom disappointed. But bridging is hot work and the water was cool and, when no bodies were in sight, we bathed and swam.

I decided that it would be nice to sail on the Ganges but as yet was not up in boat construction, so I based my design on the native dhow-like craft that we saw on the river. A folding boat about twenty feet long served as the hull, with a twenty-foot bamboo for mast and the side of an EPIP tent for a sail. We had plenty of block and tackle and ropes, and a large oar for a rudder. I reckoned that we needed a crew of about four to manage her but, in the absence of a single volunteer, I set out by myself. I hoisted the sail, which immediately filled, and the boat and I shot majestically off downstream. Now, with some difficulty, I hauled in the sail and held the rudder and changed course dramatically, but not quite enough. In the absence of a centreboard, I could not sail within ninety degrees of the wind and I saw our camp gradually retreating into the evening distance. Before I could work out the manoeuvre to beach the boat, my faithful sergeant was setting out to the rescue in one of the motor boats.

One evening the alarm spread up from another section a hundred yards downstream that a man had disappeared. He had fallen in off a pontoon and never came up again. I dived off the pontoon and swam down. For six feet the water, though dark with sediment, allowed enough light to see and then it turned into an opaque and ever thicker, slimier mud in which you could only grope. I went on searching further and further downstream until utterly exhausted. I felt that in the next dive I must gulp down some of the ghastly smothering mud and never be seen again. The body was never found and, as he was known to be a swimmer, it was thought that he must have been pulled down by a turtle.

Mongyr was a railway town and had a strong anti-British element. By now, the United States had thrown their enormous energy, manufacturing capacity and organising ability into the war effort, at last turning the tide in the Allies' favour, so the Japs were no longer a serious threat to India. As a result, the local youths became much bolder. In the town, they tended to occupy the whole pavement and, with words like 'English officer thinks he is God,' force the same into the always filthy gutter. This happened once too often in the presence of a group of large and fit African askaris, resentful of their officer's treatment, and at least one youth was laid out in the gutter. We expected serious trouble and even put another lot of concertina wire round the camp and made the town out of bounds. After a while we started walking out again to find circumstances dramatically changed. Youths gave officers right of way and a respectful, civil greeting.

We received a warning that it was raining in the hills and we ought to return our equipment to the depot upstream. But we were very happy here and thought we would stay as long as possible. Next day the river had risen a few inches but so what? The next morning it had not only risen a foot but was visibly rising as we watched. We quickly made two large rafts with the pontoons. Loaded with the rest of the equipment, each raft, driven by four outboard engines, just about held its own against the current. With a motor boat towing each, we began to make some progress, but soon the ever-rising river defeated us. We had not trained in vain: we dropped four anchors from one raft and with two motor boats reached the landing beach with the other. There was still a further problem, however. By the time we arrived with the second raft, the beach was a foot deep and all the equipment had to be winched up a twenty-foot bank. As the last pontoon reached the top we looked back over the sacred river, now a three-mile wide roaring torrent. Miraculously, the only casualty we suffered was one pontoon—perhaps a small cost compared with the wisdom we had acquired.

We now moved to another temporary camp in fairly wild sandy grass country. This time we had tents but had to construct loos and our own water supply, which task was left in the hands of an ex-Rhodesian copper mining engineer. The loos were ingenious. First he dug a twenty-foot vertical shaft and then, from the bottom of this, a horizontal tunnel four feet high and thirty feet long. The hard-packed sand needed no supporting. Using a six-inch earth auger, he made ten holes from the surface to the tunnel, each with a wooden surround. As it happened, they were never used, for their fame spread abroad and every day parties of generals, colonels and all ranks from engineer companies came to view them, including a trip down by ladder. Before the tourist season was over we had moved again.

The well construction was also simple. Forty-gallon drums (in plentiful supply) had top and bottom removed, then the smallest askaris available, with the aid of a bucket, dug out a cylindrical hole into which the drum was dropped, and so on, drum by drum, until the water table was reached at about thirty feet.

For some reason I shared a tent with a nice dental officer whose name, for a more obvious reason, I always remember. He was Captain Hacking.

Chapter Twelve

Before the now famous loos could be used, we moved to another camp near Ranchi. Here the whole East African Division was spread in hutted camps over a great area of plain. It was rumoured that the division was likely to take part in a seaborne landing in South Burma and we were training hard with this in mind. By now, equipment was more easily available and we were gradually getting our G1098 (official inventory of equipment) complete. At least we had real mine detectors and were confident that we were an efficient fighting unit; most were keen to be allowed to have a go.

On 7th May 1945 we were sitting in our mess. All around was dark and still, except for several African drums keeping up a constant rhythm. Suddenly we were listening as if we had heard something. In fact what we heard was silence, as all the drums had stopped. Then we picked up quite a different, excited beat in the far distance, which spread like wildfire until every askari in the division spread out over the plain was beating furiously on anything that came to hand.

About an hour later we had an official signal from Brigade HQ to say that Germany had unconditionally surrendered. The war in Europe was over. The Japanese war machine was still in full swing but surely now, against the undivided might of the Allies, it couldn't last out much longer? Meanwhile, we were ever more in a state of readiness.

The EA Mule Company was about a mile from our camp and, apart from the pack-transport mules, it had a number of horses for the use of officers and mule handlers. The CO had an idea that Europeans were better than Africans at exercising horses and offered anyone who wished a ride each morning. I took this up enthusiastically and was again excused PT. The exciting part of the exercise was that the horses, commandeered from all over India, were very different in character and each morning we were issued with a different one. Sometimes it would be a lazy old hack that only moved under extreme protest; another day one might have a beautifully trained polo pony. Once I had a wild, almost unbroken youngster. After an impressive demonstration of bucking, we were easily first out of the compound and across the plain, decidedly out of control. I managed to guide him into a deep *nullah* (dry water course), hoping it would slow him down. It did—but then he decided to leave the *nullah* via a long knife-edge of compacted gravel, along which he led almost the whole field, miraculously without injury.

The officers in our field company were now getting on well together. I was senior subaltern and when the second in command was posted, I took over his job with the rank of temporary Captain. This was entirely an administrative office job, to which I didn't take at all kindly. I would have much preferred to have remained a platoon officer but thought my parents would be disappointed if I ended the war in such a lowly rank. Remarkably, the African office clerk could *almost* always read my writing and was most polite about my spelling. 'Did you have a special reason for spelling it this way, Bwana?'

In India there was not always quite the same respect for truth as (there used to be) in the West. On one occasion, my African MT sergeant went out to deal with a broken-down truck and found he had to return to the camp for a spare part. He was a good man and I had no reason to doubt his story, especially as none of his tribe were involved. Having collected the part, he returned to the site of the accident, unfortunately by himself. He was travelling quite fast when an Indian, whom he thought was under the influence of some drug, staggered out from behind a pile of stones right in front of his truck. He braked but couldn't stop until after he had run over the man with front and back wheels. Fairly sure that the man was dead and that at the time there were no witnesses, he thought he had better take him to the military hospital. While he was trying to lift him into the truck a crowd, attracted by the screech of brakes and cloud of dust, arrived and started hurling stones at him, so he leapt in and returned to the camp to report to me.

No doubt I should have made out a written report in triplicate, but instead I reported it in person to the nearest Indian police station. Nothing happened for three weeks. Then I was sent for by the DAPM, who demanded to know why the accident had not been reported to the police, who denied all knowledge of any report. He then handed me ten typed and thumb-printed documents, saying, 'You have got yourself into this mess, you had better get yourself out of it.'

Despite the seriousness of the situation, I had to smile at the reports. They were identical 'eye-witness' accounts of how the truck had come along at the speed of a flying goose, had deliberately run over the man, who was on the side of the road, and had driven on non-stop at the same anserine rate. It was difficult to understand how illiterate Indians, unable to sign their own names, had correctly read and recorded the make and number plate of the 'flying goose'. Still, I was very loth to subject my sergeant to an Indian court on a charge of, at least, manslaughter. After a night spent in as much thought as sleep, I sent for the sergeant.

'Sergeant, how many askaris of your tribe were in

your truck at the time of the accident?'

In rather an offended voice, 'But I told you, sir. I was by myself.'

'You have seen these ten reports, haven't you, Sergeant? How many of your tribe were in the truck?'

The offended expression slowly faded, a smile started in his eyes, spread to a great grin and, as can only happen in an African, enveloped his whole body. From somewhere down in his boots came a deep chuckle.

'*Kumi na mbili, Bwana.*' (Twelve, sir.)

Without further prompting, I was soon in possession of twelve signed statements, in broad agreement but with slight individual variations in the telling. I was almost convinced myself that they must be genuine eye-witness accounts and I handed copies to the DAPM. The documents were never used as by now the Japs had surrendered and, to his great joy, my sergeant was sent back to Kenya. The local police were informed that if they required him as a witness they must pay his return fare. This was obviously the best solution, though by now I had begun to look forward to demolishing the Indian witnesses.

In August 1945 two of the newly invented atomic bombs were dropped, Russia declared war on Japan and the Emperor unconditionally surrendered. On the ethics of dropping the bomb, I think that Laurens Van der Post (see *The Night of the New Moon*) is right in believing that it actually saved thousands, if not millions, of Allied and Japanese lives. The Japanese military machine, once started, could never have admitted to a military defeat until the last Japanese fighting man was dead; in the process all military and civilian prisoners and countless Allied service men would have perished. A technical defeat, however, was out of their control and 'face' was not lost.

It was wonderful, of course, that at last the war was over but in a strange way some of us were bitterly disappointed. In my case, I had been training for six long years and at last was all ready to go in with a company that was fully equipped and prepared for the job. Now came a definite anticlimax. Here we were suddenly, with no object except to get back home and restart our lives but with no chance at all of leaving India in the foreseeable future. There were millions of Allied fighting men under arms thousands of miles from home but the war had decimated our merchant navy and the current generation of transport planes or converted bombers could not possibly cope. It seemed also that the East Africans were at the very bottom of the priority lists, especially in this sector, where US forces were at the top.

Traditionally, soldiery in a foreign land with nothing to do causes trouble. It would be six months before a ship was available to return the division to Africa and we had to find ways to keep ourselves busy. One solution was the staging of a Great African Searchlight Tattoo. This was particularly good for the EAE who had the job of producing the grandstand and props. My responsibility was to make a troopship to steam on to the arena and disembark units of the 11th EA Division. With the help of a tank transporter, wood, canvas, paint and searchlights, the result was impressive.

Two things from the Tattoo stand out in my memory. First, a mass askari PT display in perfect time without the aid of any shouted orders, or even a drum. Quite uncanny until one realised that the leading gymnast was on top of the spectators' stand, out of sight of the audience. Second was an animal dance by members of one of the semi-desert tribes. It was hard to believe that the animals were really humans, very especially the ostriches who strutted about on long thin legs with a human arm making an amazingly realistic head and neck.

I was also much involved in the Mounted Sports, so called for some technical insurance reason. My brief was to lay out a racecourse with hurdles and a betting enclosure and to put up competition jumps. The Royal Engineers Pocket Book, not surprisingly, was no help, so details of height and construction of jumps had to be empirical. For this purpose, I had a horse sent round from the Mule Company and constructed jumps at the height that he could just get over. When the day came, I borrowed the same horse and entered him for the show jumping, knowing that he could clear them. Unfortunately, the old horse also knew that I had built the jumps to be easily collapsible and in his excitement went straight through rather than over every one. In the steeplechase he did his best, but it wasn't quite good enough.

We tried hard to keep the askaris interested. As none of us relished playing at soldiers for its own sake, we confined military subjects to the mornings and left the afternoon to sport and 'rehabilitation'.

The latter included brick and pan-tile making, for which purpose we employed an Indian craftsman. I can see him clearly now, sitting cross-legged in front of an old lorry wheel with a lump of clay on it. He would spin the wheel with his feet, deftly pulling up the clay to form a perfect cylinder which he cut in two with a wire.

We also had a reading and writing class for illiterates and I gave a simple maths class for the innumerates. I think this taught me more than the class; it certainly showed me that I am not a born teacher. Having found simple mathematics very easy, I was just not prepared for some of the class who found the concept of adding, subtracting and multiplying on a blackboard meaningless and impossible to grasp. Yet, given the practical exercise of shopping in rupees with change in annas, they managed very well.

At long last we had orders to hand in all but personal equipment to the Indian Ordnance Corps and to be ready to leave at a moment's notice. We had somehow acquired certain items (mostly picks and shovels) surplus to our G1098. These the Indian Ordnance Officer refused to accept, though any shortages caused no worry. When I asked what I should do with the surplus, he suggested digging a hole and burying them, which seemed a terrible waste of good tools. I would rather have sold or given them to the local villagers but, as the accountable officer, I felt sure this would get me into trouble. In the end we dumped them, under cover of darkness, outside the Ordnance Officer's mess.

The scheduled day came for us to board a train for Bombay but, owing to riots at Calcutta, this had to be postponed for forty-eight hours. Because of the subsequent railway chaos, we were running seventy-two hours late before we reached our destination. The system was to take our own hard rations but to stop at various stations for tea made by the Indian Service Corps. On arrival at one such station, I was met on the platform by an Indian lance-corporal who saluted smartly.

'Are you the Train Adjutant Sahib?' he asked.

I said that I had this title.

'I have tea ready for you. In fact I have had it ready for three days.'

To prove his point, he took me to a huge bubbling cauldron of coal black liquid. It appeared that the milk had gone off and the sugar had been pinched, but the latter didn't matter as we had our own. The European officers and NCOs wouldn't touch the stuff but the Africans classed it *chai mxuri sana* (absolutely wonderful tea).

Chapter Thirteen

There must have been moments of great beauty and joy on the voyage, with the shipful of men, returning after years away from home, ploughing through the equatorial seas. The warm starlit nights, free of the eternal black-out and the constant nagging fear of lurking submarine packs, must have been intoxicating.

In fact, my only lasting memory is of hours spent in the stifling airless sweat of the troop decks. The askaris had acquired money in Ceylon and India, and even some English money on troopships, mostly in small change, sometimes filthy and almost indecipherable. It all had to be counted, down to the last pi (twelve to the anna, sixteen annas to the rupee), the current exchange rate worked out and this paid out in East African shillings. Then, worst of all, the transaction was entered in the man's pay book and signed by an officer (me). My never too beautiful signature was completely ruined by such signing of libraries of pay books in a hot sweaty hold. These small savings meant a lot to them and I reckoned that I was almost overpaid, so we always made it up to the nearest coin above. When the last shilling was paid out, I was about £35 down and presumed this would have to come out of my pocket (about a month's pay) but when I came to closing the company accounts there was an old NAAFI account, about which we did not know what to do, of nearly the exact amount.

The ship, though still under contract to the War Office, was already preparing for its peacetime role and on the officers' cabin deck there were several stewardesses. On an evening visit to the bathroom, clad as usual only in my pink check sarong, I was stopped by a deputation of stewardesses who ceremonially pinned a home-made sporran on the appropriate part of the sarong.

On arrival at Mombasa, I was summoned to the captain's deck. I couldn't imagine why as, for once in my army career, I wasn't burdened with any cloud of guilt and could not think of any recent behaviour out of keeping with a perfectly conventional officer and gentleman. It turned out to be dear Russ Wollen, who was in Mombasa on business and had come to welcome me home and ask me to come to Updown at my first opportunity.

As a large part of the 11th Division had arrived on the troopship, top brass decided to have a Great Triumphal March through Nairobi. For this purpose almost all the rolling stock of the East African railways had been concentrated at Mombasa. The resulting train must have been a mile long, with two huge double-bogie engines at front and rear and one in the middle. Even so, when we reached the great escarpment the speed dropped to one mile per hour and everyone got out and walked. My accommodation for the night was an eighth part of a cattle truck which, I am glad to say, had been well cleaned after its last rightful occupants. After a troopship in the tropics, it was very comfortable.

After the Great March, we entrained for Nanyuki

where I was to supervise the disbanding of the field company. However glad we were that the war was over, it was still a little sad disbanding a unit that had taken years to build up, where officers, NCOs and askaris had learned to respect each other and work together. And then there was the question of how all these men, who for up to six years had been away from their homes and families, living completely different lives in foreign lands, were going to settle down to tribal life. One of my jobs was to provide each askari with a reference that might help him get a civvy job. In practice, unless you knew the officer giving these references, they were almost useless. There were three officers in charge of disbanding three companies at Nanyuki. One was a very kind man, who thought it unfair not to give every askari a good report; one was a colonial who said that only the very best would ever get jobs and only gave the few really outstanding men a good reference. I tried to give each as true a report as I could, which took rather longer.

Off duty, life was carefree and fun. My beloved Mick came back (I believe he had been quite happy on Mu's farm, living as one of a pack, but seemed very pleased to see me again) and on many evenings we went out to supper together to various farms. Sometimes he would ride on the tank of my motorbike or, if we got a lift out, we would walk back together. On weekends I generally managed a ride and was glad to find that Mick hadn't lost his seat in the last two years.

I managed to get to Updown for a few glorious days' leave. Having had some reason to go to Nairobi on duty, I had an army truck and driver and, as Ann wanted to stay with Mu, it seemed ridiculous not to take her back to Nanyuki with me. In the general post-war euphoria, I hoped I wouldn't be court-martialled.

At last my field company was wound up and I was ready to go. I had mixed feelings about going home. When the war ended, I had sent for my engineering books and tried to get back to where I left off at Cambridge but I found it hard. I felt it would be necessary to start again in the first year and, even when the three years were over, I would probably have to spend months in an office. On the other hand, I was still lacking in self-confidence and badly wanted a university degree behind me. Then there was the effect of the media. During our time in SEAC, the only paper we read was a free copy of a weekly edition of *The News of the World*. This contained very little news but gave us the impression that almost every pretty girl had gone off with the American GIs, whom we already realised we could not hope to match financially. In many ways, it seemed infinitely preferable to stay in Africa. I had fallen in love with it and was fairly certain of being able to get a practical engineering job with the Kenya Public Works Department. Of course, we had to return home to be demobbed and it was exciting to think of seeing our families and homes again after four years.

My name came up to take the train to RAF Kisumu. At least this time orders were no longer secret, so I was able to say goodbye, or perhaps *au revoir*, to my Kenya friends and have a second, very painful parting from Mick. At Kisumu we learned that we were to be flown up to Cairo by courtesy of the South African Air Force, who were en route to bring back their own troops. They had a fleet of six Dakotas, probably the safest planes ever made, but their method of flying wasn't entirely confidence-making. They would take off from the rough dirt airstrips in line ahead, as if they were scrambled fighters, and even when airborne would suddenly dive to tree-top height to look at game. This proved a little unnerving as those of us used to driving the dreadful old cobbled-together Kenya trucks associated any change of engine note as a warning of imminent disaster.

After landing nose to tail and refuelling at Juba, we flew on to Wadi Haifa. Here our pilots were told that Egypt had been cleared of South African service-men and they were to return to South Africa. This caused them considerable anxiety—not because they had to abandon us at a small airfield in the middle of nowhere but because they had brought up loads of fountain pens, obtainable in South Africa, to flog to the troops in Cairo. We could have bought haver-sack-loads at bargain price but at the time the desire to get home outweighed financial gain and, anyhow, a fountain pen hardly seemed a romantic present after four years' absence.

How we were to get the 700 odd miles to Cairo was far from clear but accommodation and food were laid on. I walked down to the papyrus beds by the Nile and was rewarded by an unusual sight: I was watching a gecko on the path a few feet ahead of me when a snake, about six feet long, shot out of the reeds and wrapped itself round the gecko. I threw something at it and it shot off again, leaving a very dazed gecko to crawl off into the swamp.

Next day, an RAF cargo Dakota came down to refuel and offered to take four of us amongst the cargo. Being one of the four longest away, I accepted the lift. It was not uncomfortable and we could see out of the portholes well enough to witness a great sandstorm below, which luckily moderated in time for us to land safely at Cairo. At first, we were confined to barracks because of riots but next day I was able to revisit the unsurpassed Tutankhamen relics.

A few days later we boarded a US liberty boat troopship at the ancient port of Alexandria. These liberty ships were mass-produced by assembly-line prefab methods and went some way to making up the appalling loss of Allied merchant ships from U-boats, pocket battleships, mines and bombing. Without the backing of American industrial muscle, there was no way we could have stood up to the Nazi armed might.

Of course, with the mass-mobilisation of men, inevitably there were a few bad ones. Having been brought up in the army 'country right or wrong' tradition, I had been very shocked to find British officers who used their position to feather their own nests but perhaps there was more excuse for the US Forces, who were more remote from war. Whatever, this liberty ship certainly had more than its fair share of bad 'uns.

The Med was exceptionally rough and our little ship made heavy weather of it, the screw roaring and shuddering with every wave. We arrived twenty-four hours late at Malta, where ships have to pick up a buoy, an operation I have seen done with apparent ease by a British crew. This time, though, we had to make four runs while the crew stood and argued.

Troops were packed into tiny cabins, with two sets of three-tier berths, which I found rather claustro-phobic. Soon after leaving Malta, while it was still

rough, the 'heads' got blocked, causing faecal material to swirl down the passages and slop over into the
cabins. This was reported to the captain, via the OC
troops. Unbelievably, the answer came back, 'It is
Sunday and the ship's carpenter isn't working.' Eventually the situation was put right by some RE volunteers and a piece of wire.

We were also always hungry, with the main meal
of the day consisting of a slice of bread and marge,
a slice of beetroot and a mug of cocoa. When we
looked through a porthole to the crew's mess, we saw
mouth-watering Cordon Bleu meals of roast meats
and chicken. It appeared that on British troopships
rations were supplied, while on American troopers
the purser was given a cash sum for each man. But no
one returning home after years abroad was going to
risk putting in a complaint that might detain them for
weeks in Toulon. I later met an officer who reported
that the food on the outward journey, on the same
ship, was quite adequate.

We were not sorry to disembark at Toulon, where
we boarded a train. It was mid-March and Europe
was in the grip of severe frost, with snow blanketing
the whole of France. Matters were not improved by

a fracture in the steam pipe, which meant that our compartment had no heating at all—and we were dressed for the tropics!

I would like to have recorded a dramatic return to my native land at Folkestone but after crossing France and the Channel I was too cold even to think, no doubt suffering from extreme hypothermia. I seem to remember the natives speaking English and a cup of tea from the YWCA before packing into another train. After eight hours fug-up in an English train, I recall marching up icy streets at about four in the morning, followed by a delicious sleep. Then, after a day of documentation and re-equipping, I was issued with a travel warrant to Chapel station and, after four years, I was home at Baggaretts.

Postscript

Jack did not return to Kenya to work, nor did he go back to Cambridge to complete an engineering degree. Instead, still undecided about the future, he visited a careers office and worked his way through the alphabetical possibilities:

> *Agriculture seemed possible, but Baggaretts was not a viable size and there was not the family capital to buy a larger farm [...] Forestry was attractive but it seemed that after a lifetime growing trees you had to cut them down again. Medicine was certainly appealing, but I would have to overcome my squeamishness and I did not feel that I wanted any more responsibility for life and death. Then, right at the end, I came to Veterinary Medicine and Surgery; immediately I knew that this was to be my profession. It was a real Damascus Road experience and I could not imagine why it had not occurred to me before.(In retrospect, years later, I wondered if this was a subconscious atonement for the guilt I felt at shooting the zebra.)*

In October 1946, at the age of 24, he began a five-year course at the Royal Veterinary College in London.

His sister Blanche, now married to Peter Proby, asked her sister-in-law to keep an eye on Jack. Peggy Proby was studying music in London and sharing a flat with friends; the young vet student became a regular supper guest. One Sunday he and Peggy were planning a bicycle ride.

In a Semtex flash, against all reason, I knew that my life must be linked for all eternity with this lovely woman. It only remained to convince her of this undeniable fact. Emotion had outstripped all reason: what possible chance had I of persuading this girl with the world at her feet? What had I to offer? Marriage with four years on a minimal student grant followed by years in a two-up, two-down house over a surgery, probably smelling of tom cat.

Jack claimed to have proposed under every tree in Hyde Park before he was accepted. They were married in July 1948.

His first permanent post as a qualified vet was in Guildford at a salary of £8 a week. By then, he and Peggy already had a son, Harry; their daughter Barbara was born in Guildford in 1952 and their twin sons, Peter and Thomas, two years later. In 1954, Jack accepted a post in Shaftesbury, with the prospect of becoming a partner in six months. In fact, after just three, the owner decided to sell up and move to Canada. Jack was offered the chance to buy the practice and the house where it was based, near Park Walk.

At last I had what I had worked for for eight years, my own practice and the family growing up in a quiet and charming market town, and here the story should end 'and they all lived happily ever after'.

For Jack, it really was close to 'happy ever after'. After the nomadic army childhood and his war years abroad, life as a country vet suited him admirably. He writes about it very entertainingly in the later chapters of his memoir, with a collection of anecdotes worthy of James Herriot. Despite the hard work, early financial insecurity and antisocial hours, he enjoyed working with animals and, with rare exceptions, their owners. Being part of the Shaftesbury community was also a source of continuing satisfaction: he and Peggy contributed greatly and were much loved figures in the parish.

His engineering skills remained in evidence and he was constantly devising imaginative solutions to practical problems at home and at work. He also taught his family to sail and built a boat—much more successfully than on the Ganges. Off-duty hours were spent dashing down to Poole harbour to take out the Wayfarer.

Once the children were adults and the practice had grown prosperous, he and Peggy were able to indulge in the occasional exotic holiday. In 1985, when he had semi-retired, they fulfilled his long-held dream and went to Kenya, where he retraced his steps of forty years before. They stayed at the Muthaiga Club in Nairobi and with

Ann near Nanyuki, and visited the polo ground and Ten Mile Camp before setting off on a safari. Jack resumed his love affair with Mount Kenya:

> Man has always lifted his eyes unto the hills but there is something extra special about Mount Kenya. It rises out of the great hot equatorial plains through a green cushion of cedar and bamboo forest, ending in bare peaks and glaciers. For most of my army service in Kenya I was within sight of this mountain until its lure and mystery became an integral part of my life. To me it was the Land of Beyond '... that dreams at the gates of the day/Alluring it lies at the skirts of the skies, and ever so far away', as described by Robert Service (whom I consider a rather neglected poet and not only because he is almost certainly the author of 'Eskimo Nell').

Jack retired fully a year or two later. Despite a heart attack, a double hip-replacement and the onset of blindness—all in his seventies—he remained determinedly independent, generous, open-minded and always greatly interested in the world at large and his grandchildren in particular. His delightful sense of humour stayed with him to the end. Only the death of Peggy in August 2004 undermined his equanimity. He died the following year, having collapsed while walking on Park Walk, overlooking the Dorset countryside he had loved and worked in for fifty years.

Index